OPPORTUNITIES

in

P9-CSC-801

Hospital Administration Careers

OPPORTUNITIES

in

Hospital Admnistration Careers

REVISED EDITION

I. DONALD SNOOK JR.

New York   Chicago   San Francisco   Lisbon   London   Madrid   Mexico City
Milan   New Delhi   San Juan   Seoul   Singapore   Sydney   Toronto

The *McGraw-Hill* Companies

Library of Congress Cataloging-in-Publication Data

Snook, I. Donald.
    Opportunities in hospital administration careers / by I. Donald Snook, Jr. — Rev. ed.
      p.   cm.
    ISBN 0-07-146768-8 (alk. paper)
    1. Hospitals—Administration—Vocational guidance.   2. Hospitals—
Administration—Vocational guidance—United States. I. Title.

RA971.S66   2007
362.11068023—dc22   2006006200

Statistics Canada information is used with the permission of Statistics Canada. Users are forbidden to copy this material and/or redisseminate the data, in an original or modified form, for commercial purposes, without the expressed permission of Statistics Canada. Information on the availability of the wide range of data from Statistics Canada can be obtained from Statistics Canada's Regional Offices, its World Wide Website at http://www.statcan.ca, and its toll-free access number 1-800-263-1136.

1 2 3 4 5 6 7 8 9 10 11 12 13 14 15 16 17 18 19   DOC/DOC   0 9 8 7 6

ISBN-13: 978-0-07-146768-1
ISBN-10:   0-07-146768-8

Interior design by Rattray Design

McGraw-Hill books are available at special quantity discounts to use as premiums and sales promotions, or for use in corporate training programs. For more information, please write to the Director of Special Sales, Professional Publishing, McGraw-Hill, Two Penn Plaza, New York, NY 10121-2298. Or contact your local bookstore.

This book is printed on acid-free paper.

CONTENTS

8. Educational Preparation 81

Formal training. Graduate curriculum programs.
Undergraduate programs. Selecting an educational
program.

9. Getting the Job 89

Networking. Preparing your résumé. The cover letter.
Successful interviewing. Follow-up and accepting the
job. Doing well in your first job. The outlook for jobs.
Diversity in health administration.

Foreword

CAREERS IN HOSPITAL administration offer exciting challenges and opportunities. The work is important, demanding, and personally rewarding. You work with dedicated and talented people in providing vital human services. You deal with complex management, financial, and social problems. Hospitals function at the center of our nation's health-care system, and individuals who want to assume leadership responsibilities in creating the well-managed community hospitals of tomorrow will find rewarding careers.

Opportunities in Hospital Administration Careers will assist you in choosing a career in the field. Collectively, hospitals are among our largest employers and offer many dynamic career options. The book points out that the health field, especially in the past decade, has experienced tremendous growth and that jobs in health administration are exciting but also call for a great deal of knowledge, stamina, and patience. People who succeed in hospital administration combine excellent people skills with management skills. The critical challenge is to ensure that given the available resources, patients receive high-quality health care in the most appropriate setting.

I have worked with health-care executives in Pennsylvania and throughout the United States and have found them to be capable leaders with strong commitments to public service in providing health-care services to their communities. I hope readers of this book will be motivated to further explore the varied and expanding opportunities in hospital administration careers and succeed in this important work.

John A. Russell, M.H.A., FACHE
Lecturer, School of Public Affairs, Penn State–Harrisburg
Former CEO, Health Alliance of Pennsylvania

INTRODUCTION

WELCOME TO THE health-care revolution. Health care stands at the nexus of business, government, and not-for-profit organizations, and perhaps more than any other institution, it influences the quality of our daily lives. Taken as a whole, it is one of the most dynamic fields around today and presents myriad opportunities for administrators as well as medical personnel.

Advancements in technology, procedures, and medications provide us with better care and healthier lives than ever before, but those advancements must be reconciled with patients' ability to pay, cooperation from HMOs and insurance companies, and the budget realities of state and federal governments. U.S. health-care costs reached $1.6 trillion in 2003. Increases in health insurance premiums are in the double digits year to year, the percentage of provider costs covered by Medicare is creeping down, and forty-five million Americans—many of whom are full-time workers—don't have health insurance. At the same time, one-third of American hospitals are losing money, and big-ticket lawsuits have pushed physicians' liability insurance through the roof.

Administrators are the ones who must sort out the demands of all these parties while observing three important caveats: do not sacrifice quality of care, protect the system's solvency, and invest in the infrastructure. This is not an easy task.

Yet daunting challenges beget numerous opportunities. Good administrators, those who know how to work within the system while also improving it and who are as adept with people as they are with budgets, have unlimited potential in health care. More than one hundred thousand people work in health management positions today, and through 2012 demand for them will grow faster than the average for all industries in the United States.

Although hospitals will continue to employ the most medical and health-services managers in that span, employment will grow the fastest in practitioners' offices and in home health-care agencies. Many services that hospitals provided previously will continue to shift to these sectors as more care is done on an outpatient basis, especially as medical technologies improve. Managers with specialized experience in a particular field, such as reimbursement, should have good opportunities.

The Business of Health Administration

Health administration in general, and hospital administration in particular, engages in many of the same activities that most commercial enterprises do. In the health administration business, however, the administrative and service functions found commonly in commercial enterprises are integrated with a host of additional complex activities—for example, laundry, power plant engineering, dietary service, maintenance, and a variety of technical nursing and medical care activities. This makes hospital administration a challenging, innovative, and demanding profession. The health-care administrator must be concerned with people, programs and services, and facilities and equipment.

Just as our health-care system has become more complex, so has the role of the key decision maker—the health service administrator. Health-care institutions have become more specialized and more sophisticated, and accordingly so has the administrator's role. At one time, nurses could move up through the ranks to hospital administration; in church-related hospitals, it was common for the administrator to come from the religious order or perhaps from the retired clergy. It was also a common practice to promote the hospital's business manager or accountant to the chief administrator's job or even to recruit a retired businessman or a retired physician to assume the position of administrator. Those days have passed.

Health-care administrators do, however, have the power to improve the quality of care and make a difference in patients' lives. For example, an analysis in *Hospitals & Health Networks* magazine in 2005 revealed that the United States' "most wired hospitals"— those that have invested significantly in health information technology—have risk-adjusted mortality rates that are 7.2 percent lower than other hospitals. If such strategic uses of technology can raise the bar, then surely so can the people leading the way to the hospitals and care centers of tomorrow.

1

HEALTH ADMINISTRATION: A PIVOTAL FIELD

EVEN IF YOU haven't worked in health care or health administration before, you've read the headlines and likely experienced the effects firsthand. Health care, at least the American system, is in crisis. Its costs are rising far faster than incomes, hospitals face a critical shortage of qualified nurses, and inefficiencies in delivery of care confound administrators, doctors, and patients alike.

Experts differ on the solutions, but they can all agree on one thing: quality health care is essential for all of us. The system extends far beyond hospitals and the offices of individual practitioners. It encompasses outpatient care centers, public clinics, university health centers, and assisted-living facilities. It also includes hundreds of thousands of doctors and millions more health professionals performing related work. And it benefits from one hundred thousand administrators working at all levels to improve the system, serve patients, manage costs, and interface with medical staffs to produce progressively better outcomes.

Existing structural difficulties aside, administrators' roles and responsibilities are expanding all the time. By 2030 an estimated 20 percent of the U.S. population will be sixty-five or older, the demographic that also requires the most intensive and expensive care. Well before then, doctors and researchers will have developed hundreds of new techniques, drugs, and devices to improve care. And it will be up to health-care administrators, the field's leaders, to decide how to accommodate that aging population, allocate that groundbreaking technology, and manage the usual daily operations while facing more public scrutiny than ever before.

How Health Administration Is Organized

Hospitals and, more broadly, health administration are the central components in managing health institutions and agencies. Health-services managers are recognized as professionals under the umbrella of health-services administration, including its major component, hospital administration. *Health administration* is a broad term. It encompasses various management activities, including planning, organizing, controlling, and supervising, as well as evaluating institutional and community resources, systems, and procedures by which the needs and demands of the health- and medical-care systems are met.

Management means directing various functions in an institution to help make a health organization work. In smaller operations administrators do this personally; in larger institutions they work through a staff of assistants. Health administrators are called upon to make many decisions. For example, they might approve budgets and negotiate contracts. Assistant hospital administrators might direct the daily operations of various departments, such as food service, housekeeping, and maintenance.

More specifically, hospital administrators are responsible for all of the hospital's operations and its related units, whether they manage a large urban hospital or a small rural facility. The board of trustees, the hospital's governing authority, hires the administrator and is responsible for seeing that the board's policies are carried out.

Administrative Roles

Administrators assume various roles while managing their institutions, but most will fit into at least one of three specific roles. Sometimes they fit into all of them. They might be: a business manager, an institutional coordinator, and/or a chief executive. To some degree, most administrators assume elements of all these roles.

- **Business manager.** The administrator is responsible for many of the institution's internal operations. This means that he or she must order and procure supplies, manage personnel, and provide physicians and other health-care professionals with the resources they need to do their jobs. A business manager must also deal with financial and statistical data, which are the basic reports of the hospital's financial affairs. A hospital visitor might find the administrator poring over budget reports or formulating strategies with the chief financial officer.
- **Institutional coordinator.** The administrator has to develop more of an outside role. Being a coordinator involves wielding influence as a negotiator, particularly regarding the insurance plans that pay patients' hospital bills. Being active in public relations is also

part of the coordinator's role. In this capacity administrators work with very diverse groups. They might discuss a problem with medical staff over coffee in the physicians' lounge or routinely make rounds to keep in touch with employees, patients, and visitors. Perhaps the administrator's most important tool as coordinator is communication. Communicating through writing, public speaking, and even e-mail and phone calls is important to getting the job done successfully.

• **Chief executive.** The executive role usually is reflected in the administrator's title. The chief administrator might be called the executive director, executive vice president, or president and chief executive officer (CEO). As you can see from the number of titles, the definition of health administration is quite broad. It encompasses the management of many various institutions and tasks. But all institutions have one thing in common—they provide medical and health services.

The employees, staff, board, and public have a right to expect the administrator to look the part of the executive. Administrators must be well-groomed and dressed appropriately. Their style might be conservative, as it is in many institutions, or it might be less formal. The important element is that the administrator be dressed appropriately for the occasion and that he or she relates well to staff.

The Administrator as Leader

There is a big difference between being a manager and being a leader. The health-care industry demands that health-care CEOs lead as well as manage. Managers' style and experience determine their *approach* to management, but it's their leadership that gives management *purpose* and *direction*. Here, several eminent health-care executives respond to the question, "What one characteristic is required of effective leaders?"

> *Good leaders must have vision of purpose. They need to know where they want to go, how they want to get there, and who they want to take with them.*
> —Diane M. Howard, Fellow American College of
> Healthcare Executives

> *As health-care executives, we must identify the right direction for our organizations and inspire our teams to strive toward that vision.*
> —Captain David P. Budinger, USA, Certified
> Healthcare Executive

> *A good leader must have integrity and instill it in all areas of the organization. A leader upholds the values, ethics, and mission of the organization.*
> —James E. Dalton Jr., Fellow American College of
> Healthcare Executives

> *Good leaders adapt and evolve without losing sight of their quest to move their organizations through enormous changes and challenges.*
> —Donna G. Case, Fellow American College of
> Healthcare Executives

The Dynamics of Professional Hospital Administration

Hospital administration involves many of the same responsibilities that most institutional administrators and managers handle, but hospital administration is unique because it's a complex association of professionals performing in matters of life and death. Hospitals have administrative and service functions that are common to other commercial enterprises, but they also have complex and unique services integrated with the usual departments. In a hospital you find maintenance, laundry, and power facilities alongside highly technical nursing and medical-care activities. This variety and complexity is what makes hospital administration such a demanding profession. Fundamentally, hospitals are made up of people, and hospital administrators are primarily concerned with people.

In earlier times, hospital administrators sometimes were selected from the ranks of nursing. It was common to find registered nurses serving as institutions' head administrators. In church hospitals, particularly Catholic hospitals, it was common to select the administrator from the ranks of the religious order. These earlier administrators were diligent, hard-working, and quite competent. Many administrators also came up through the ranks from the business office. Occasionally the hospital was managed by a retired businessman. The days of this type of upward mobility to the CEO level are gone.

Hospital administration's journey to professional status began in the 1930s, when an organization now known as the American College of Healthcare Executives (ACHE) collaborated with the American Hospital Association to establish a code of ethics for hospitals and administrators. ACHE demands the highest standards of education and ethics in the hospital administration profession. The

ACHE code of ethics specifically outlines how health administrators are accountable in their performance. (You can read the full code of ethics online at www.ache.org.) Today university-level programs at the baccalaureate, master's, and doctoral levels are common throughout the United States and Canada. All formal training programs for hospital administrators cover at least three general areas:

1. Administrative theory
2. Medical and health-care delivery
3. Business functions, including organization and management theory

See Appendixes A and B for information on accredited programs.

Several highly specialized professional organizations, listed in Appendix C, represent the field of hospital and health administration. In addition, a number of well-respected technical and professional journals point to the growth of hospital administration as a field. Some of these are listed at the end of Appendix C. These add to the specialized body of knowledge for the management and planning of health services.

The Physician as Administrator

Physicians have taken a greater interest in the hospital decision-making process because it affects their professional lives. Some physicians are assuming the chief executive officer's role. There are also other management roles for physicians. The hospital's medical director is usually an employee who has senior administrative responsibilities. The chief of the medical staff is another administrative physician who is responsible for coordinating the functions of the medical staff. This position provides an excellent training ground for learning supervision of personnel and resources. Larger hospitals have full-time department heads—the chief of medicine and the chief of surgery.

Doctors moving into administration face a difficult balancing act. The issues administrators handle and the perceptions they hold are different from those of doctors, and there can be questions about where the loyalties of a doctor-turned-administrator lie. Some doctors who segue into management continue to practice part-time to maintain credibility; others throw themselves into their new position and draw on their previous experience to connect with the medical staff. Conversely, administrators with business and management backgrounds sometimes discount doctors in these roles as something less than true executives. It is up to doctors who pursue management to find a happy medium, even if it means floating in limbo between these two worlds. In any case, the positions are excellent opportunities for physicians who wish to move up into CEO positions, and it's likely that more physicians will move into executive management jobs as the challenges on both sides merge and become more complex.

Inside Hospital Activities

Historically the hospital administrator's job was just to manage those things that went on in a hospital. Part of the job was to oversee all the buildings, grounds, and facilities and to see that the hospital's personnel were qualified and performed their jobs well. It was the administrator who had to answer legally for the acts of his or her employees under the principle of *respondeat superior*.

Maintaining a positive relationship and effective communication with the hospital's physicians is a key internal duty. An effective administrator has to be a competent communicator. Remember, the administrator is the board of trustee's agent and, as such, may have to monitor medical ethics and morals, as well as the hospital's rules and regulations.

Dealing with People

The administrator deals with many different kinds of people and groups. But there are several groups of individuals that the administrator must deal with regularly in the course of a day. Effectively working with these groups allows the administrator to operate the institution more efficiently. Some of the groups include the administrator's first-line supervisors, the institution's board of trustees, the medical staff, employees, patients, the public, hospital vendors, other health administrators, and governmental and other regulatory agencies.

Dealing with the Board of Trustees

The board of trustees is the governing body of the institution and gives the administrator ultimate authority. In other words, the board is the administrator's boss. It delegates to the administrator the authority to manage the affairs of the hospital or institution. The official relationship is that of employer and employee, but actually the administrator and the board function more as partners. The administrator is the representative of the board in the daily activities of the institution and should at all times be dignified and professional. Administrators attend board committee meetings as well as meetings with medical staff. Administrators make formal reports and recommendations to the board of trustees regarding the hospital's activities.

In some institutions the administrator, by virtue of the position itself, might also be a member of the board. Boards have to be directly accountable to the community and to the public served by the hospital or institution. Over the last several years, boards have been reviewing more frequently management's decisions to make sure that they comply with board-developed policies. Some of the real challenges for both the administrator and the board arise when they and the institution fall under the scrutiny of the public and mass media. (One recent example comes from the nonprofit side, where some hospital CEOs came under fire for making salaries that are on a par with those in the corporate world. A 2004 *Chronicle of Philanthropy* survey showed that the five highest-paid CEOs among nonprofits were hospital executives. CEOs at the six largest nonprofit, tax-exempt hospital systems were making more than $1.2 million a year. In another case, public relations professionals had to combat assertions that a vaccine ingredient called thimerosol, which contains small amounts of mercury, is linked to autism in children.) And perhaps the most important task before the board and administration is working together to continually improve the institution's quality of care.

Dealing with the Medical Staff

The administrator acts in partnership not only with the board of trustees, but also with the physicians and other health-care personnel. Under the best circumstances the administrator has a mutual understanding with, respect for, and trust in the members of the medical staff. One of the key responsibilities of a hospital administrator is to communicate with the hospital's medical staff. It is the administrator's job to see that the physicians have the proper tools in the right place at the right time for them to carry out their roles in the hospital.

Successful administrators must be effective in keeping their medical staff informed about organizational changes, board policies, and decisions that affect them and their institution's patients. Hospital medical staffs, though ultimately answerable to the board and its management, are also self-governing; consequently, they have their own bylaws. The administrator should be sensitive to the medical staff's needs for self-governance and support that need. From time to time natural frustrations will arise between the medical staff and the administration. Frequently the source of this conflict is poor communication. Administrators must communicate effectively with the medical staff if the hospital is to function efficiently. The administrator must be available to medical personnel for consultation as much as possible.

Dealing with Employees

Employees are the working force behind the hospital, but they also account for many of the administrator's day-to-day challenges. Personnel raise many complex human problems for administrators, who not only have to resolve these problems but also have to keep employees informed of their critical role in the hospital's success. This is easier to achieve with nurses and others who deliver direct patient care, but administrators must continually remind all employees in the hospital of their mission and importance. As they deal with employees at all levels, it is crucial that the administrator show objectivity, understanding, and fairness. The administrator must hire, direct, discipline, and dismiss employees with these important principles in mind.

Dealing with Patients and Their Families

The administrator has a vital role in public relations when meeting with patients and their families. He or she must fulfill all their legitimate requests for general comfort and care in order to assist their recovery. When dealing with patients, the administrator must also understand the patients' visitors and relatives. It is important that the administrator safeguard confidential patient information just as doctors and nurses do. Confidential information, whether from patients or staff, belongs to the institution and must not be used by administrators or others for their own gain or self-interest. In fact, no hospital insiders should use a patient's information improperly. Misuse of this material or knowledge is also a violation of the ACHE code of ethics.

Outside Hospital Activities

Administrators face a host of outside responsibilities. They must understand and participate in appropriate community activities. Staying in touch with the latest government rules and regulations is essential to the institution's sound operation. Maintaining government relations is important to the administrator. There is often a need to maintain a social presence in the community. Administrative growth can be developed by participating in continuing-education activities. The hospital administrator is the board's agent, and the board of trustees is accountable to the community; therefore, finding out what is going on in the marketplace and bringing these new changes back to the hospital is important. The CEO is expected to show leadership within the hospital as well as outside of it. The administrator has a major role in educating the community on hospital matters, which is particularly important as consumers voice concerns about rising health-care costs.

Dealing with the Public

It is the administrator's job to remain in close contact with the community that sponsors the hospital or health-care institution. The administrator has the responsibility to foster favorable public relations, which can be an important ally for the administrator in reaching the community. Just as patients' perceptions about their care often come from a doctor's bedside manner, their attitudes toward a care facility can depend on public relations messages. Messages spread through websites, brochures, and in advertising need to be consistent and also responsive to public sentiment and crises. Top administrators must be prepared to participate in TV and radio interviews and at public events continually, not only when bad news breaks.

The administrator must realize that the institution has a responsibility to the public and that the public has a right to be informed. The administrator is important in this process. How successful he or she is in this role to a large extent determines the reputation of the hospital. One way the administrator can establish effective communications with the public is by staying in personal contact with key members of the community and keeping them up to date on the institution's policies.

2

WORKING WITHIN THE SYSTEM

THE HEALTH-SERVICES or medical-care system in this country is a set of mechanisms through which human resources, health-care facilities, and medical technology are organized by means of administrative structures. This system offers integrated services in sufficient quantity and quality to meet the community's demands at a cost compatible with the community's financial resources. It is within this medical-care system that administrators find jobs. The U.S. medical-care system has five distinct elements. Four of these elements, or components, are related to specific institutions: they are *outreach*, *outpatient*, *inpatient*, and *extended*. The fifth element encompasses these institutions and is called *community at large*. Take a look at each of the components and institutions the medical-care system is associated with to get a better feel for which institutions and agencies most need administrators. Then see what settings administrators typically work in.

Outreach

Perhaps the best place to start a review of the medical-care system is the outreach component. The traditional medical-care system attempts to meet the primary medical needs of its patients through outreach programs. These programs are generally decentralized and widely scattered. One of the earliest and most common types of outreach services is that of solo medical practitioners, who have offices located in neighborhoods. Physicians with private practices provide the bulk of care to the middle class in this country, but the urban poor continue to use city health clinics and similar institutions as a substitute for family physicians. Other forms of the outreach component include neighborhood community health centers, community mental health agencies, physician group practices, and a variety of other ambulatory care arrangements including the outreach activities of health maintenance organizations (HMOs).

Hospitals also have reached out to their communities and demonstrated a new emphasis on preventive care by adding or expanding health promotion services. These educational and support services are intended to help individuals reduce their health risks, manage their health, and use health services effectively. They might be targeted at patients through patient education services or at the residents of a community who are not currently patients.

Outpatient

Another area of our medical-care system is outpatient care. One of the major institutions providing this component is the traditional hospital clinic. The growing outpatient services also include emergency facilities. Large numbers of patients use emergency rooms not just for emergencies but as primary care when they have no alternatives. Also included in the outpatient component are ambulance squads, whether they are community, municipal, or police or fireman rescue squads. Ambulance assistance is an outpatient service that has taken on increased status with the advent of paramedics, emergency medical technicians (EMTs), and emergency medical systems, such as the cardiopulmonary resuscitation teams that have saved so many lives. Physician group practices are common in larger medical centers and are also part of this outpatient category.

Even more dramatic than the decline in inpatient hospital use has been the increase in community hospital outpatient visits. The increased volume of surgical procedures done on an outpatient basis accounts for much of the growth in outpatient visits. The shift toward ambulatory surgery is not the only factor behind growth in hospital outpatient visits. Community hospitals have expanded the number and variety of outpatient services they provide.

Inpatient

The third institutional component, and the largest in terms of cost and personnel, is the inpatient component. The inpatient element is measured by the number of hospital inpatient beds. Americans have asked the country's hospitals to provide a spectrum of inpatient care ranging from very sophisticated intensive care to minimal care, and all of these types of care take place inside the hospital using hospital beds. Over the past decade, growth in outpatient services has far outstripped that of inpatient admissions. Many treatments and procedures that would have required an inpatient stay a decade or two ago now are routinely delivered in outpatient settings. As a result, fewer patients are being admitted to hospitals.

Hospitals vary by ownership, purpose, and specialty. The most common hospital is the *short-term community hospital.* There are more than fifty-two hundred community hospitals. Hospitals operated by governments, whether state, federal, city, county, or district, are called *governmental* or *municipal hospitals.* There is a third category, referred to as *specialty hospitals,* that includes long-term-care hospitals.

Extended

This is the fourth element in the medical-care system. It includes but is not limited to such services and institutions as home-health-care and hospice programs, end-stage renal-disease programs, skilled nursing facilities (SNFs), and intermediate-care facilities (ICFs). Together, the SNFs and the ICFs are known as nursing homes. There are also assisted-living facilities, personal-care residences, rehabilitation hospitals, and visiting nurse associations.

The extended component expands yearly due mainly to the growth in the elderly and poor populations, both of which tend to suffer frequently from chronic conditions. This has resulted in a shift in focus from episodes of illness (such as admissions, visits, or length of stays) to continuous, comprehensive care management.

Community at Large

The fifth and final element in the medical care system is the non-institutional component referred to as the community at large. The community is divided into three major groups. The first comprises consumers—patients who use the health-care facilities. The second group comprises health personnel needed to staff the system. This includes a variety of training programs and medical and nursing schools, as well as medicine's residency programs. Also included in this element are labor unions. Third and perhaps the most powerful part of the community component is the federal government, which pays for so much of the hospital care through the Medicare and Medicaid programs. At the same time, private insurance agencies provide coverage for the majority of employed Americans. An element that is key to the community at large is the federal, state, local, and voluntary regulatory agencies. Much of the regulatory controls are focused on quality care and cost issues. Finally, the political system—the politics of health care—is behind the legislation that governs the funding and direction of the health-care system in this country.

In this outline of the five distinct components that make up our nation's medical-care system, one thing is very clear. The system tends to be a sickness-care system more than a health-care system. HMOs and managed-care organizations were designed to change this way of thinking. Each of the medical-care components is part of a complex array of institutions and programs that involve people and countless other resources. And, needless to say, these institutions and programs must be managed. It is the administrators of hospitals and managers of health-care services who will perform these important managerial tasks.

Specific Organizations and Where Administrators Work

The following list shows a breakdown of the types of organizations and programs in which administrators working in the medical field can be found.

Hospitals and Hospital Systems
Corporate office specialists
Functional/department managers
Senior hospital administrators
System executives

Long-Term Care
Adult day care
Home-care agencies
Hospice programs
Nursing homes

Care-Related Areas
Ambulatory care services
Group medical practices
Managed-care organizations and insurance companies

Other Areas
Association work
College teaching
Consulting
State and local health departments
University health services research

(See Appendix D for sample job advertisements.)

3

WHAT IT TAKES

MANY OF TODAY's health-care institutions and organizations must be in top running order night and day. In those institutions the staff must be thoroughly trained and the facility ready for any emergency that might arise. Though hospitals and other provider institutions are primarily concerned with the sick, they are also businesses and must be operated efficiently. It is the administrator who is held accountable for managing the hospital. Such a formidable task requires certain skills.

Necessary Skills

A profile of a successful health-care administrator indicates that he or she must have a mixed array of technical and professional business skills. The basic skill requirements for a health administrator parallel those for most executive management jobs, but there is the added responsibility of understanding health-care systems. The health administrator must be able to manage people, finances, and materials. The modern manager must be both creative and cost effective. An accomplished administrator must have three basic types of skills: technical, interpersonal, and conceptual. He or she must also be able to take on new administrative skills as necessary and all the while maintain effective leadership.

Technical Skills

The health-care administrator must be proficient in specific types of business methods, procedures, and techniques in addition to possessing specialized knowledge of analytical tools. Administrators are required to run a modern-day health-care institution. Obviously such job responsibilities require that the administrator be an extremely good organizer. Within the hospital, for example, there are members of the medical staff and perhaps hundreds of other employees who must be effectively organized. Further, there is a need to understand and develop systems. Frequently the administrator must formulate rules and regulations that govern the hospital. Administrators should have a working knowledge of personnel and business administration and an understanding of the role of public relations in the institution. Expertise in planning has become more important as hospitals have grown. Also an understanding of financial management and reimbursement systems is absolutely necessary to keep the institution fiscally solvent.

Interpersonal Skills

The administrator must be able to work effectively as a team member and promote cooperation among the other members of management. The successful administrator should also have very good human relations skills and be able to use discretion and good judgment when called for. This is especially important since administrators deal frequently with a variety of people including doctors, nurses, engineers, accountants, patients, and visitors. The successful administrator must produce an aura of satisfaction for the complaining patient, relative, or employee. The tone of cooperation in dealing with employees and medical staff is set by the administrator. This requires tact, diplomacy, and seriousness. A sense of humor is also important. Perhaps the most important skill is the ability to work with people. The administrator will find varied, difficult problems to solve among groups including, but not limited to, the board of trustees, the medical staff, patients, and assorted personnel. Problems must be resolved for the hospital or health-care institution to operate effectively. As in any business, being an accurate judge of human nature is a valuable asset.

Conceptual Skills

The administrator must be able to see the institution in a broad perspective. Where the institution fits into the community must be understood, and the institution's contribution to the economy of the community must be appreciated. Administrators must understand the political, social, and economic forces that affect the institution. With this understanding and sensitivity, the administrator is expected to lead the hospital or health-care institution as well as be a leader within the community at large. The administrator must understand broad health issues and then offer a vision to the institution of how to cope with them.

The combination of technical, human relations, and conceptual skills required to be a successful administrator is important today in managing varied and complex health-care institutions.

New Administrative Skills

Since hospitals are changing so rapidly, new skills are always in demand. A customer (patient) orientation, an entrepreneurial spirit, and adaptive skills are some of the new skills needed. Elements of customer orientation include guest relations programs, local business and industry programs, and the physician's role. Since the majority of patients are directed to the hospital by physicians, the institution they choose is the one that creates an atmosphere that makes their lives rewarding, pleasant, and satisfying. Administrators who support customer orientation are invariably successful.

Also key to being a successful administrator is an entrepreneurial spirit. Those administrators who do best are those who, using their instincts, aggressively seek new ways of improving their hospital and gaining a competitive advantage. Successful administrators, to survive and prosper in an uncertain and competitive world, are continually adjusting their management style to adapt to the environment.

Effective Leadership

Health-care organizations are undergoing unprecedented change. At this time it is more critical than ever for managers to know where the organization is headed—in other words, the vision for the organization. What is needed from today's health-care manager is effective leadership. What does it take to be a successful leader in health-care administration? Success in leadership requires risk taking, imagination, and a willingness to trust and engender trust. Especially important in health-care management is the ability to work within and motivate teams of people. Effective leadership means pulling together and motivating team play and team success.

Effective managers are not solo acts. Often it is the leader's task to select the best people and then turn them loose.

Activities and Tasks

Health-care administrators perform a variety of tasks and functions, and quite naturally these vary with their institution and specific job assignment within that institution. The senior administrators in hospitals and other health-care institutions are referred to as the *chief executive officers*. The other managers and assistant administrators within the organization must work with and support the chief executive officer's objectives and goals. This is called *team play,* and it is critical in health-care management. It is important to understand how the chief executive officers operate and what they do in the course of a day's work.

The hospital administrator of the 1950s and 1960s was primarily concerned with the internal operations of the hospital (that is, the planning, organizing, supervising, and controlling of the hospital's operations). This frequently involved bargaining with employees and determining the best systems and methods to internally manage the institution. Today, however, the administrator assumes dual responsibilities inside and outside the hospital. The chief executive officer has become more involved in activities outside the institution. The modern health-care executive must strike the proper balance between inside institutional activities and outside activities.

Inside Activities

Traditionally it has been the hospital administrator's job to see that the hospital's buildings and facilities are in adequate running order and that the employees are qualified for their specific jobs. In fact, legally, it is the administrator who must answer for the acts of the employees under his or her supervision. Another traditional function of the hospital administrator is to interface with the physicians on the medical staff. The administrator has the responsibility of keeping the physicians informed about the important happenings in the hospital and its plans. Further, the administrator traditionally has had the responsibility of keeping the hospital's governing body, the board of trustees, informed.

Generally, the administrator must attend board meetings to communicate ideas, thoughts, and policies that will help the hospital. Financial management is a traditional responsibility for administrators, too. They prepare and defend annual budgets to be approved by the board of trustees. This includes identifying new services that need to be offered as well as new equipment that needs to be purchased. Negotiating reimbursement rates and contracts with managed-care organizations and preparing monthly financial statements and statistical data that are presented to the board are among the internal tasks performed by an administrator.

The inside activities can be grouped under duties that include the review and establishment of hospital policies and procedures, supervision of the hospital and its operations, and dealings with employees. The administrator must establish the proper working conditions and environment for employees and see that the morale of the staff is maintained at a high level. Finally, the administrator is responsible for ensuring that the hospital is well furnished with the supplies and equipment required to treat patients. Additionally, the administrator must make sure that the building is maintained in safe operating condition and that adequate sanitary conditions exist.

Outside Activities

The outside activities of today's administrator are numerous. They include relating to the community, understanding governmental relationships, and participating in outside educational opportunities and joint planning activities with other health-care providers. One of the roles of the modern administrator is to educate the community about hospital operations and health-care matters. This might be done through the hospital's website, a press release, a brochure, public address, or a media interview. It is the administrator's responsibility to present a positive image of the hospital. Public relations duties are considered key outside activities, and the administrator must encourage an understanding of the hospital's programs by using the mass media. One of the most valuable accomplishments of today's administrator is the negotiating of contracts with third-party payers (insurance companies) who pay for the patients' bills. This is a time-consuming activity requiring a combination of robust management and negotiating skills.

Modern hospital administrators direct and coordinate the activities of their institutions. They take on the role of promoting favorable public relations not only within the community but also among the hospital employees and staff. Administrators must see that the hospital continually updates its buildings and equipment. They also must coordinate the activities of a variety of personnel and groups, including the medical staff and the board of trustees.

How Administrators Spend Their Time

Today's hospital executives spend their time on a wide range of activities. Responsibilities involve planning, controlling, organizing, directing and coordinating, operating, and "extramural activities": in other words, serving as the public face of the institution. These responsibilities include health industry activities, internal education, public and community relations, information systems, financial and business management, physical facilities and equipment oversight, team management, meetings, policy and strategy, personnel management, legal and governmental compliance, clinical service operation, administrative research, and medical-center operation.

A survey by the *Journal of the Academy of Hospital Administration* found that the largest portion of an administrator's time, 30 percent, was spent engaged in health industry activities. Other major duties, each accounting for roughly 10 percent of an administrator's workload, were supervision of departments; internal education; policy and strategy; and administrative meetings. With the exception of finances, the remaining responsibilities, such as information systems, administrative research, and, surprisingly, hospital operation, each occupied less than 5 percent of an administrator's time. Of course, each day wouldn't break down this neatly. The big-picture nature of a high-level administrator's responsibilities mean these percentages settle out over weeks and months, not day in and day out. So what happens when? The ability to discern what needs attention and to prioritize are two indispensable qualities of any effective health care executive.

Nature of the Work

As you can see, the administrator's job is not an eight-hour, nine-to-five position. Because the administrator is concerned with all phases of the hospital's operations, he or she is frequently out of the office keeping track of hospital activities. Frequent visits must be

made to the various hospital departments. And since the administrator is called upon to be the institution's representative to the public, he or she may be found addressing various civic or fraternal
groups. Energy, good health, and vitality are essential to someone
in this position. Because much of the administrator's work involves
dealing with people and showing patience, an even temper is also
a valuable asset.

Advancement in the Field

It should be clear by now that it is very unlikely that a graduate
directly out of college or even recently out of a graduate program
in health-care administration will move immediately into the chief
executive officer's job in a hospital. Administrators advance in the
profession by gaining experience in management activities and
building a successful record of accomplishment. This is commonly
done by taking jobs in a hospital that offer experience in one or
more areas of specialized administration, for example, working as
a department head in charge of purchasing or personnel. Beginners
should gain experience in budgeting, handling employees, supervision, and reimbursement systems. After building a track record at
lower-level management positions, the administrator will generally
seek promotion to successively more responsible positions, perhaps
as an administrative assistant, then assistant or associate administrator. In some instances, administrators begin their careers outside
the hospital field proper and then enter at a top-level management
position, but this is not very common. Eventually, regardless of the
specific career path, most administrators ultimately hope to be the
chief executive officer of their organization.

4

HOSPITALS AND
TOP ADMINISTRATORS

HEALTH CARE IS one of the largest industries in the country, and hospitals represent the largest fiscal component of this industry. But changes are affecting hospitals as never before. After a dip in the number of admissions to U.S. hospitals in the mid-1990s, 2003 saw thirty-six million people admitted as inpatients, a figure on a par with rates in the mid-1980s. At the same time, outpatient visits have continued their robust rise as ambulatory care centers shoulder an ever-greater burden of day-to-day treatment.

Hospital mergers and consolidations continue in virtually every geographic area of the country. Running a comprehensive-care facility is tremendously expensive, and those that are market leaders and have the greatest financial resources have a distinct advantage. Mid-market hospitals and those in rural communities often struggle to compete and face either consolidation or outright closure.

Types of Hospitals

All hospitals are not alike. They might have different purposes and different functions. Essentially, hospitals take care of a patient's medical, surgical, and psychiatric needs including illnesses and injuries. The work varies hospital by hospital. The kinds of medical and health personnel that work in hospitals differ by type of hospital as well. The basic differences between hospitals lie in how they are classified. Fundamentally, a hospital can be either a community hospital or a noncommunity hospital. Our hospital industry is a mixture of both private and public hospitals.

Hospitals have different types of ownership structures as well. They might be organized for different purposes. Some are organized as voluntary (nonprofit) hospitals; others are organized to make a profit. Hospitals can be governed by community representatives or owned by religious orders. They can be general medical-surgical hospitals or specialty hospitals. And they can be differentiated by how long patients stay. Some hospitals are noted for medical education and teaching. Others have no teaching or research facilities. The American Hospital Association classifies hospitals as one of four types:

1. **General hospitals.** The primary function of the institution is to provide patient services, diagnostic and therapeutic, for a variety of medical conditions.
2. **Specialty hospitals.** The primary function of the institution is to provide diagnostic and treatment services for patients

who have specified medical conditions, both surgical and nonsurgical.

3. **Rehabilitation and chronic disease hospitals.** The primary function of the institution is to provide diagnostic and treatment services to handicapped or disabled individuals requiring restorative and adjustive services.

4. **Psychiatric hospitals.** The primary function of the institution is to provide diagnostic and treatment services for patients who have psychiatric-related illnesses.

Hospitals are also classified by who owns or controls the institution. The different control classifications are:

1. Government, nonfederal

   - State
   - County
   - City
   - City-county
   - Hospital district or authority

2. Nongovernment not-for-profit

   - Church
   - Other

3. Investor-owned (for-profit)

   - Individual
   - Partnership
   - Corporation

4. Government, federal

- U.S. Air Force
- U.S. Army
- U.S. Navy
- Public Health Service
- Department of Veterans Affairs

The primary mission of a hospital is patient care; however, there are others. An important one is the training and education of doctors, nurses, and other health professionals. Yet another is clinical research. Typically, larger institutions have carried out these functions. Today hospitals are the focal point for the entire community's health care, offering a vast array of outpatient services as well as traditional inpatient care. With this emphasis on outpatient treatment, hospitals have taken on an increasing role in preventive medicine. They have become the places in many communities where physicians, nurses, and other health-care professionals pool their efforts to improve the public health of the community as well as treat illness. Public education as a means of improving public health is an important responsibility of the community hospital.

There are many kinds of hospitals. The most common is the voluntary not-for-profit hospital, commonly referred to as a community hospital. Of the nearly six thousand registered hospitals in the United States, 85 percent are community hospitals. Their prominence is even greater when viewed in terms of patients served. In 2004, 95 percent of admissions in registered hospitals took place in community hospitals. There are two major categories of community hospitals: the teaching hospital, where nurses and doctors are trained, and the nonteaching community hospital. University hospitals and large medical centers are teaching institutions that emphasize education and research as well as service. These hospitals usually have very sophisticated clinical services.

The federal government and state and local governments also operate hospitals. Some are community hospitals, but the federal government generally provides care for specific groups, such as military personnel, veterans, or even government employees. Many state and local hospitals are involved in psychiatric care and special health services for the poor. A smaller number serve institutions, such as prisons or universities.

Finally there are investor-owned (for-profit) hospitals. These hospitals are owned by investors or private individuals for the purpose of gaining a return on their investment. These hospitals are usually community hospitals, though there are many proprietary psychiatric hospitals. Community hospitals are generally referred to as short-term, general, or acute hospitals. Generally, patients are admitted to these short-term community hospitals for fewer than three weeks. Long-term hospitals, which often administer psychiatric care, may well keep patients a month or longer.

Inpatient care as a whole, however, has fallen out of vogue because of the overhead costs associated with modern hospital stays. As costs have risen on both sides, hospital administrators have responded by redesigning many procedures as outpatient affairs and accomplishing more with a smaller staff. Across the board, patients are frequenting overnight hospitals less and spending less time there when they do. Delivering mothers know this; births that a few decades ago warranted a stay of several days now have mother and baby out after one night. Tellingly, the number of beds in community hospitals fell 29 percent between 1983 and 2003, during which time outpatient visits rose 137 percent and total staff grew by 25 percent. Despite the decline in the number of hospital beds, as well as hospitals themselves, expenses have continued their precipitous climb. Expenses at community hospitals during this twenty-year stretch rose 265 percent, to $500 billion. Table 4.1 offers a general sense of where all this money comes from. Private households accounted for 32 percent of the expenditures for all health care and associated products—not just hospital costs—in 2003, on a par with government and business.

Hiring the Chief Executive Officer

It is the board of trustees' responsibility to hire a competent, well-trained hospital administrator to lead the hospital. This might be the most important single task a board has to perform. Before hiring an administrator, the board undertakes a search (often seeking outside assistance) for the best person to lead the institution. Since hospitals are big business, trustees frequently seek administrators who have skills in business disciplines, including planning, organizing, and controlling (or managing the plan). Communication and leadership skills are also strongly desirable. Upon hiring the administrator, the board delegates authority and responsibility for the institution's day-to-day operations to him or her. However, the trustees must retain the ultimate responsibility for what occurs in the hospital. The formal relationship between the board of trustees and the administrator, or chief executive officer (CEO), is an employer-employee relationship. Successful administrators develop a partner relationship with their board. It is the board's responsibility to guide, counsel, and evaluate its administrator and, if necessary, to terminate him or her.

Table 4.1 Expenditures for Health Services and Supplies, by Type of Sponsors, 2001-2003

Type of Sponsor	2001	2002	2003
	Amount in Billions of Dollars ($)		
Health services and supplies	1,373.8	1,499.8	1,614.2
Businesses, households, and other private	862.9	923.4	992.2
Private businesses	369.3	395.1	423.0
Households	442.4	475.4	512.6
Other private	51.1	52.9	56.6
Governments	510.9	576.4	622.0
Federal government	278.1	318.3	344.0
State and local governments	232.8	258.1	278.1
	Percent Distribution		
Share of health services and supplies	100	100	100
Businesses, households, and other private	63	62	61
Private businesses	27	26	26
Households	32	32	32
Other private	4	4	4
Governments	37	38	39
Federal government	20	21	21
State and local governments	17	17	17
	Average Annual Percent Growth from Previous Year		
Growth of health services and supplies	9.0	9.2	7.6
Businesses, households, and other private	6.2	7.0	7.4
Private businesses	7.8	7.0	7.1
Households	5.8	7.5	7.8
Other private	-0.4	3.6	6.9
Governments	13.8	12.8	7.9
Federal government	17.4	14.4	8.1
State and local governments	9.9	10.9	7.7

Source: Centers for Medicare & Medicaid Services, Office of the Actuary, National Health Statistics Group, 2005.

Hospitals are complex institutions. The governing body of most hospitals, as we have learned, is the board of trustees, also known as the board of directors, which is led by a chairperson. It is the board's responsibility to head up the hospital, set policy, and select and hire the chief executive officer or administrator. The hospital is usually organized into major divisions, including the support, professional, fiscal, administrative, and nursing divisions. The hospital administrator, who might be called president or executive director, is hired by the board of trustees and is responsible for all aspects of the hospital's daily operations and division functions.

Usually the administrator relies on the physicians' and the medical staff's judgment in patient care matters and works closely with the chief of the medical staff. Most hospital administrators are specially trained for their position. Many university graduate programs offer a master's degree in health administration. There are also undergraduate programs that train hospital administrators.

Senior Administrative Staff

One of the most important responsibilities of the chief executive officer is to select and hire a competent administrative staff. It is the administrator's staff that is delegated the responsibility of seeing that the hospital is run smoothly and efficiently. Some of the key senior administrators include chief financial officer (CFO), chief nursing officer (CNO), chief operating officer (COO), and chief medical officer (CMO). The hospital also includes department managers in the many nonmedical departments, such as personnel, medical records, dietary control, housekeeping, and purchasing. The purchasing agent, frequently called the materials manager, is also a key department head who must order supplies to maintain logistical support within the hospital. The public relations director is an important part of the management team and the board in reaching out to the community. The personnel director, now usually called the human resources director, is critical in selecting and orienting hospital personnel as well as guiding the hospital administrator on personnel matters. The hospital business manager and controller are also key individuals in maintaining the hospital's financial records. The management information department and its manager have become a very important ingredient in the modern hospital. See Figure 4.1 for a sample organizational chart.

Job Summaries and Compensation

Here's a closer look at the types of responsibilities and salaries of some of the key senior administrators in hospitals.*

Chief Executive Officer (CEO)/Administrator

- **Job summary.** Responsible for overall functioning of organization and for adherence to organization's mission. Develops and implements strategic plans for maintaining and/or improving delivery of services.
- **Median compensation.** Base salary—$268,000 (total cash $313,200)

Chief Operations Officer (COO)/Administrative Officer

- **Job summary.** Responsible for day-to-day operations carried out by the organization. Acts in place of CEO/administrator when CEO is not available.

---

* Source: 2005 Hay Group Hospital Compensation Report.

Figure 4.1 Sample Organizational Chart

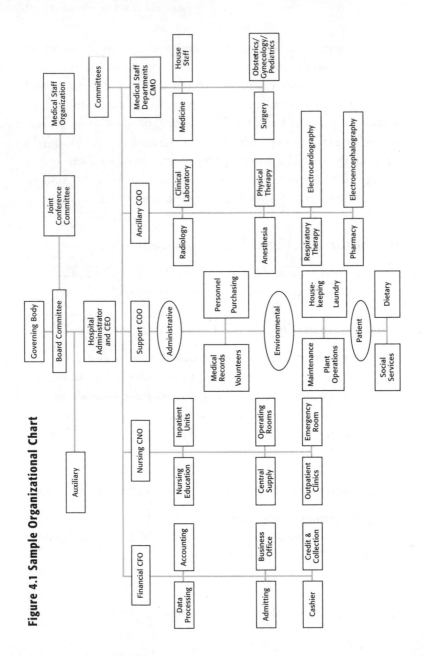

- **Median compensation.** Base salary—$166,400 (total cash $186,800)

Chief Financial Officer (CFO)

- **Job summary.** Responsible for developing and implementing organization's financial plan and for implementing accounting and budgeting policies. Directs processes whereby departments develop budgets, track expenses, record and collect revenue, and maintain financial statements.
- **Median compensation.** Base salary—$160,000 (total cash $179,300)

Chief Medical Officer (CMO)/Medical Director

- **Job summary.** Directs medical staff planning, recruitment, and development. Acts as liaison between administration and medical staffs. Implements organization's policies with respect to delivery of medical services.
- **Median compensation.** Base salary—$241,200 (total cash $248,400)

Chief Information Officer (CIO)

- **Job summary.** Provides strategic and tactical planning, development, evaluation, and coordination for the institution's information and technology systems. Responsible for the management of multiple information and communications systems and projects, including voice, data, imaging, and office automation.

- **Median compensation.** Base salary—$134,200 (total cash $135,700)

Patient Care Executive/Chief Nursing Officer (CNO)

- **Job summary.** Serves as frontline executive overseeing and enhancing patient care. Must build relationships with medical staff, recruit and manage nursing staffs, and ensure that approaches to care align with the institution's strategic goals. Responsible for nursing budget.
- **Median compensation.** Base salary—$138,800 (total cash $152,500)

5

DEPARTMENTAL ADMINISTRATORS
IN THE HOSPITAL

THE OPPORTUNITIES FOR administration in a hospital are not limited to the few executive jobs at the top; many other challenging and diversified management jobs exist in today's hospital. Because of rapid, continuing growth in the health-care field and the trend toward specialization, many new administrative positions must be filled to effectively operate today's hospital. Scientific and medical gains have had an impact on all health professions and occupations, including those in management. Some management positions do require a degree of technical knowledge, but many can be learned with a combination of formal schooling and on-the-job experience. One example is the executive housekeeper. Other administrative jobs offer specialists practical experience in their primary occupations and the opportunity to manage people and other resources.

Nurses, pharmacists, accountants, and many other professionals are all candidates for this type of administrative position.

Certain key hospital departmental administrative positions will be reviewed by following the general functions of a hospital as outlined in the typical hospital organization chart in Chapter 4. The managerial positions are divided into four general categories: finance, support and administrative services, management in nursing service, and planning and marketing. Specific positions under each category are listed here.

Finance
Hospital controller
Director/manager of accounting
Director of admissions
Data processing manager
Director of managed care
Director of compliance

Support and Administrative Services
Director of human resources
Purchasing director/materials manager
Food services administrator
Executive housekeeper
Director of volunteer services

Management in Nursing Service
Chief nursing officer
Case manager
Risk manager
Quality assurance director

Planning and Marketing
Director of marketing
Director of public relations
Director of development

Administrators in Finance

The majority of the financial management specialist's duties focus on financial analysis. The financial management specialist is also responsible for accounting and capital, department budgeting, and auditing.

Managing a hospital's finances involves more than just keeping track of what funds come into and go out of the institution. The hospital administrator has to know at all times how the hospital is operating as a business. Quality of care must be maintained at high standards. Appropriate fees must be charged for services of all degrees of complexity. Knowing the appropriate amount to charge for service is an administrator's job, and financial managers carry out the responsibility of these decisions. Financial management is part of the detailed system that establishes appropriate fees for services and determines how they should be recorded and reported.

Because many hospitals do not operate to generate a profit as most retail businesses do, there are many unique, interesting aspects of hospital financial management. Many traditional business systems that are used in a purely profit-making business might not be appropriate in the nonprofit hospital. This added dimension means that the men and women who select hospital financial management as a career must be bright, motivated, and innovative.

The administrators who manage the monies in the hospital keep the institution alive. With proper management of funds, the hospital is able to pay nurses and doctors, provide services to the community, purchase needed medical supplies and equipment, and continue to add to its buildings and facilities.

There are administrative careers at all levels of hospital financial management. They include the following.

Hospital Controller

The controller is the head of the fiscal division of the hospital and is responsible for the entire area of the institution's financial management including budgeting, bookkeeping, general accounting, crediting, and collecting on patients' bills. The controller generally reports directly to the hospital administrator. Reporting to the controller are several financial department heads, including the business office manager, the accountant, and the hospital's patient accounts manager. Having delegated certain key responsibilities, the controller spends time establishing appropriate financial reporting and accounting systems. The controller might work closely with both the hospital administrator and the board of trustees, informing these parties of the institution's financial status and its outlook.

To accomplish job duties, the controller works closely with the various hospital departmental managers. As part of the job, the controller recommends different ways to improve the fiscal operation of their departments, including recommendations to increase revenues and decrease costs.

Educational requirements and skills include a bachelor's degree in accounting or business administration as the minimum educational requirement. Experience after college in progressively responsible accounting or finance positions, preferably within a hospital, is also needed. Some supervisory responsibility would be helpful, as would course work in hospital administration. Certain hospitals might require state certification as a certified public accountant (CPA). Often controllers have been promoted from the position of senior accountant or business office manager.

The average salary is $92,900.

Director/Manager of Accounting

This position might also be called *manager of patient accounts* or *credit manager.* The person doing this job supervises the patients' accounts branch of the hospital's financial area and coordinates and supervises the hospital credit and collection department. The credit manager or members of the staff direct the institution's collection effort by interviewing hospital patients, both inpatients and out-patients, and determining their ability to pay for the services they received or might receive. Facts and information are gathered during a credit interview that relate to the patient's pay scale, present job, past credit record, and any debts or loans the patient might have. The credit manager might also run various credit references on the patient. It is the manager's responsibility to explain the hospital's credit and collection policy to the patient or next of kin and then, if necessary, to aid the patient in working out a payment plan.

Educational requirements and skills include a college degree or some college courses in either business administration or accounting. Several years' experience in credit and collection work is preferred by most hospitals.

The average salary is $79,700.

Director of Admissions

The admitting officer might be the first employee the patient has contact with when coming to the hospital. The admitting officer is in charge of the admitting department and is responsible for supervising and coordinating all the departmental operations. The department head usually works with assistants called *admitting clerks*. One of the manager's main functions is to select, train, and supervise the admitting personnel. The department is held accountable for all the various steps a patient must go through prior to being admitted to the hospital. The admitting staff assigns the patient a room, notifies other hospital departments of the admission, and takes all the administrative and clerical data for the patient's medical record. The admitting staff also explains the hospital's rules and procedures to the patient and might obtain signatures on certain release or permission forms. The department must keep current information on patient room assignments and transfers.

Educational requirements and skills include a college degree in business administration or a social science. One or two years of prior work in an admitting department are required. Some hospitals might employ a nurse as the admitting officer.

The average salary is $74,800.

Data Processing Manager

The manager of the hospital's data processing department is responsible for coordinating all of the department's functions. This department uses computers and other electronic data processing equipment and applications. The operations of the data processing department are constantly changing because of improvements in computers (hardware) and computer programs (software). The functions of this department are quite complex. One of the major functions of the data processing manager is to advise management on new information systems and to inform the other hospital department heads about the various financial and statistical reports generated from the data processing area. The data processing manager is responsible for all three main functions in the department: the planning, programming, and processing of data and information.

Educational requirements and skills include a bachelor's degree in computer science, accounting, or mathematics. Some experience in programming and systems work is also helpful. Several years' experience in computer-related work will generally be required before assuming the manager's position.

The average salary is $95,200.

Director of Managed Care

This administrator directs and coordinates the development of managed-care strategies and activities for a medical center and its affiliates. This person advises and consults with operating departments to handle managed-care requirements in terms of utilization review, billing, and registration. The director also coordinates with practice groups and clinical departments managed-care opportunities for specific services and programs such as employee assistance programs, occupational health, and substance-abuse services.

Educational requirements and skills include a bachelor's degree in business, finance, health-care management, or a related field. An M.P.H., M.H.A., or M.B.A. or M.P.A. degree with a health-care concentration is preferred. Experience working with physicians and managed-care plans; solid knowledge of managed-care contracting requirements, various reimbursement models, and government regulations; and the ability to negotiate contract arrangements with physicians, vendors, and payors are also desired.

The average salary is $95,900.

Director of Compliance

Hospitals and health-care organizations face a great number of regulatory requirements from state and federal governments and must also comply with certain independent organizations' standards. Directors of compliance ensure that all departments meet these requirements and standards, such as HIPAA (the Health Insurance Portability and Accountability Act of 1996) and JCAHO (Joint Commission on Accreditation of Healthcare Organizations), by implementing the necessary policies and practices. They must stay current on new legislation and policies that might affect hospital operations.

Educational requirements and skills include a bachelor's degree and at least seven years' relevant experience in the field. Many have master's degrees.

The average salary is $89,600.

Administrators in Support Services

The support services in a hospital represent the functions that support the medical and nursing divisions in the institution. The support services include three general functional areas: environmental services, including the housekeeping and maintenance departments; administrative services, including the personnel and purchasing departments; and patient-service areas, including the pharmacy and social services departments. All the support departments require detailed management if they are to operate efficiently and contribute to the hospital's mission of patient care. The following is a selected list of administrative positions available in the hospital support services.

Director of Human Resources

This person manages the hospital's personnel department functions. This department head is responsible for the recruitment, selection, and placement of employees within the institution. The personnel director has the responsibilities of developing personnel policies and procedures on working conditions, employment practices, pay scales, and grievance procedures. The personnel department is also responsible for providing employee orientation programs and establishing training programs.

Educational requirements and skills include a bachelor's degree with a major in business administration, personnel administration, or industrial relations. Work toward a master's degree will enable a person to advance more rapidly. Courses in tests and performance measurements as well as applied psychology are helpful. The ability to analyze job situations and to effectively communicate with people is important in this position.

The average salary is $93,000.

Purchasing Director/Materials Manager

Purchasing is a basic function in any business. However, in the hospital business it takes on greater dimension and importance. Hospitals need a wide variety of supplies, materials, and equipment because of the range of clinical situations handled in the institution. In the hospital field there is also constant change and growth in the number, kind, and sophistication of medical supplies and equipment. The pace of change in this area is probably faster than in any other industry. This means the job of a hospital purchasing director is stimulating and exciting. The purchasing director is responsible for supervising and directing a program to purchase the necessary supplies, materials, and equipment to keep the hospital functioning properly. This involves supervising the storage, control, and issuance of supplies to the various hospital departments. The director must also maintain contacts with the hospital's vendors and keep up to date on prices, trends, and the availability of supplies and new products.

Educational requirements and skills include a degree in business administration or a related field. Courses in accounting, marketing, and purchasing are helpful. Knowledge of applied business economics and business practices is also desirable.

The average salary is $84,200.

Food Services Administrator

In some ways hospitals are very much like large restaurants. They must prepare and serve meals to patients and staff. But unlike restaurants, the food prepared in the hospital may well play a role in a patient's recovery. Many developments have occurred in dietary research over the last fifty years. Science has given us new tools and methods to measure people's food needs. It has shown us the role various nutrients play in making us healthy.

The food services administrator might also be called the administrative dietician. It is this department head's job to direct and coordinate the food preparation for the hospital. The manager is also responsible for the preparation of special diets for patients. Responsibilities also include supervising personnel, requisitioning food and supplies, and maintaining records.

Educational requirements and skills include a college degree in nutrition, business administration, or a related field. Being familiar with large-scale food operations such as those found in universities and hospitals is also necessary. An understanding of quality controls in the purchasing and preparation of food is desirable.

The average salary is $69,600.

Executive Housekeeper

There are very few things more important in the day-to-day administration of a hospital than keeping it clean. The supervision and direction of the institution's housekeeping program is the responsibility of the executive housekeeper. The person in this management position must set the standards of cleanliness throughout the hospital. Establishing work methods and systems, preparing cleaning schedules, and hiring and training the housekeeping department employees are part of this administrator's job. The hospital's laundry service might also be part of this person's responsibility.

Educational requirements and skills needed for this position include a high school diploma in order to be certified for membership in the National Executive Housekeepers' Association. College courses in management are also helpful. Knowledge of the hospital's operations and a thorough understanding of building materials and equipment are important in this position. Supervision of employees is a key part of this manager's role.

The average salary is $57,700.

Director of Volunteer Services

There has been a significant role expansion for hospital volunteers over the last several years. Volunteers are no longer restricted to working in the hospital snack bar or to manning the hospitality cart. Today's volunteers can be found in all areas of the hospital—covering the telephone switchboard, serving as patient-care representatives, acting as substitute mothers in the pediatric unit, and generally supporting the hospital in its mission. Volunteers are also found working on outreach projects and serving under the auspices of a hospital auxiliary to aid the hospital in fund-raising activities. This army of volunteers needs a manager to recruit, train, place, and manage in the context of the hospital's overall mission.

The director of volunteer services, or the director of volunteers, directs and coordinates the effort of the volunteers in the hospital. To do this, the department head must establish a volunteer program in conjunction with the various hospital departments that use volunteer services. The director of the volunteer department organizes formal instructional programs for volunteers to orient and teach them proper hospital procedures and techniques. At times this departmental administrator will suggest and supervise projects to be completed by the volunteers.

Educational requirements and skills include a college education. It could be helpful to have taken courses in management, sociology, and psychology. Training in public relations and public speaking are very helpful in this position. Most hospitals prefer that their director of volunteers have some supervisory experience, have experience as a volunteer, and/or have participated in some community organization work.

The average salary is $52,200.

Administrators in Nursing

Nursing in the modern hospital is carried out in separate areas called nursing units. The organization of the nursing unit is an achievement of many years' development. The person in charge of the nursing unit is called the *head nurse*. The responsibilities carried out by the head nurse are broad and complex, for a nursing unit is a microcosm of the entire hospital. The head nurse must carry out policies and procedures, cope with crises with patients and staff, attend to routine floor administration, and relate to the patients' visitors.

To help the head nurses in their management of the nursing units, some hospitals employ unit managers or floor managers.

Chief Nursing Officer

The top nursing officer directs nursing staff planning, recruitment, and development. This person coordinates activities of the nursing staff with those of other areas, implements the organization's policies with respect to delivery of nursing services, and oversees the nursing budget.

Educational requirements and skills include a master's degree—M.S.N., M.B.A., M.H.A., or a related degree. A candidate who has not served as a CNO previously should have at least three to five years of upper-level management experience in health care.

The average salary is $138,800.

Case Manager

The case manager identifies inpatients who are at high risk of readmission and works with these patients during their stay to help them achieve maximum independence once they have been discharged. The manager works with other members of the healthcare team to develop the multidisciplinary care plan (critical paths) and coordinates with social workers to arrange community support services for high-risk patients following discharge. He or she also provides support and couseling to patient and family.

Educational requirements and skills include a degree as a registered nurse and a minimum of at least two to four years of clinical experience.

The average salary is $59,500.

Risk Manager

The hospital has a great deal of liability for clinical practice. This has been established by the courts and laws of various states. The hospital has a duty to keep its patients free from harm. To reduce the hospital's liability and also to provide a safe environment for its patients and staff, hospitals use a logical and systematic approach called a *risk management program.*

The hospital risk manager is a member of the administration who works closely with the nursing service and the nursing units. It is the manager's job to implement and coordinate the institution's risk management program. The manager uses insurance company reports, hospital incident reports, licensing and accrediting agencies' surveys and audits, as well as his or her own inspections to structure ways the hospital can lower its risk and improve its environment. Orientation and training sessions for staff are part of this person's role.

Educational requirements and skills include a bachelor's in nursing, health care, or other clinical field. Accounting/finance might also be acceptable. A background in both patient care and risk management or in a legal setting is desired.

The average salary is $73,700.

Quality Assurance Director

The concept of quality assurance has been well established in manufacturing industries for many years, but only recently has it been adopted by hospitals. Considerable attention has been placed on quality in medical care by consumers and review agencies. The courts have also placed hospitals on notice that they must ensure the quality of care in their institutions. As a result of the Medicare law, hospitals started utilization review programs in 1966, and, later in the 1970s, began medical audit programs. These are two major components of a hospital's quality assurance effort.

The quality assurance director, who might also be called a utilization coordinator, is in charge of the hospital's quality assurance program. This department head will maintain a system of control over the utilization of the facility, including monitoring the patient's length of stay and the appropriateness of services the patient has received. The department will publish criteria for medical audit and reviews. The director will work with the various hospital and medical staff committees to review and improve patient care. The manager will retain records and profiles on patient care and utilization studies performed.

Educational requirements and skills include a bachelor's degree or a master's degree and generally at least seven years of relevant experience. These directors might have degrees in hospital administration or a related field such as nursing. A broad knowledge of medical terminology is required.

The average salary is $82,600.

Administrators in Marketing

The reality for hospitals is that health care is a business and finances remain an administrator's most pressing concern in the industry today. Marketing, then, is indispensable in promoting the hospital's expertise, attention to patient care, and value to the community through every available means, including advertising, surveys, public relations, and internal communications. Fund-raising, though a smaller operation, also often falls under the banner of marketing, given its blend of PR and marketing.

Director of Marketing

The marketing and program planning specialist is responsible for projects and tasks relating to market research, planning, and promotion; interpretation of patient/customer/physician attitudes, values, and expectations; assessment of current programs; and testing of the clinical, operational, financial, ethical, medical, and legal feasibility of proposed programs. Services that may be provided include those involving high-tech equipment, medical programs such as organ transplantation, burn centers, airborne medical evacuation services, and hospice programs.

Educational requirements and skills include a bachelor's degree and ten years or more of experience in the field.

The average salary is $96,400.

Director of Public Relations

The director implements the organization's community and public relations activities, including advertising, marketing, and press releases.

Educational requirements and skills include a bachelor's degree and a minimum of seven years of PR experience, preferably with prior management experience.

The average salary is $78,200.

Director of Development

It is the job of this communication and fund-raising specialist to develop programs that will increase the amount of political, community, and financial support. Other duties include planning and implementing fund-raising efforts, such as specific projects and activities that are a part of annual or capital campaigns, as well as evaluating fund-raising programs.

Educational requirements and skills include a bachelor's degree and five to ten years of fund-raising experience. This position requires excellent communication tools and techniques and the ability to assess constituency, consumer attitudes, expectations, and level of support.

The average salary is $82,100.

6

Administrators in Related Areas

Now that we have reviewed administrators in the hospital setting, we will look at some other health-care organizations and work settings that are available for health-care-related administrators.

Health-Care-Related Organizations

There are a variety of health-care settings that employ administrators, including the following.

- Multihospital and integrated delivery systems
- Group practice management
- Management service organizations
- Managed-care organizations
- Ambulatory services
- Behavioral medicine and mental health
- Long-term-care institutions

- Insurance companies
- Consultancies
- Other health-care agencies

Multihospital and Integrated Delivery Systems

Entities made up of two or more hospitals, more commonly known as multihospital systems, supply many opportunities to today's managers. These systems no longer operate only hospitals but also nursing homes, psychiatric hospitals, health maintenance organizations, preferred provider organizations, and other freestanding facilities. When a hospital system broadens its range of services in this way, they are referred to as *integrated delivery systems.* The management team of multihospital systems plays important roles in financing and marketing its subsidiaries' services and acquiring goods and services for them as well. Multihospital systems continue to increase.

Group Practice Management

A medical group practice is a formal association of three or more physicians and possibly certain other health-care professionals, such as optometrists, podiatrists, nurse practitioners, and physical therapists, who provide patient services. The income generated initially from this medical practice is pooled and then redistributed to the group members under some prearranged plan. Often these associations are partnerships or a legal entity known as a professional corporation. The group practice concept is beneficial to doctors, since by grouping together they save on various overhead expenses in running a practice. Group practices can be organized in different ways.

The larger groups require business managers or administrators to aid them in their practice. A group practice may even own its private clinic facility. Business managers of group practices may belong to the Medical Group Management Association, formerly known as the National Association of Clinic Managers.

Like the hospital administrator, the medical group practice manager must be familiar with both finances and patient accounts. Handling records and procedures as well as understanding personnel administration is important in this job. Also, the professional medical group manager is involved in a great many matters related to the medical staff. The concept of group practice should continue to grow since it is quite difficult for a solo practitioner to keep up with the current technology, health-care regulations, and ever-changing methods of reimbursement. And, as in so many growth industries, there continues to be a demand for qualified administrators.

Management Service Organizations

Health-care organizations everywhere are recognizing the competitive necessity and high value of leveraging administrative services to physicians through management service organizations (MSOs). In addition to the professional management of routine medical office functions such as billing and accounts receivable, the MSO can be of enormous help in tackling the many challenges of managed care. For the MSO to be successful, it must negotiate often thorny politics, earn the acceptance and support of a diverse medical community, build an excellent infrastructure, and be cost-efficient. Offered services vary dramatically from one MSO to the next, but virtually all MSOs include some electronic infrastructure.

Managed-Care Organizations

A managed-care organization (MCO) refers to any type of organizational entity providing managed care, such as an HMO. The first public appearance of the term *health maintenance organization* was on March 23, 1970, when the Department of Health, Education, and Welfare presented a health-cost-effectiveness bill to the House Ways and Means Committee. There was no specific organization outline at the time, but rather, a general concept of a health maintenance contract. Later, in 1973, a report from the Committee on Interstate and Foreign Commerce launched what would become the HMO Act, Public Law 93-222. At that time an HMO was legally defined. An HMO is responsible for providing most health- and medical-care services required by enrolled individuals or families. These services are specified in the contract between the persons or family enrolled and the organization company, the HMO.

There are more than five hundred HMOs with sixty-five million members. Popularity of HMOs differs by region. The northeastern United States is a historic stronghold, while they've been less popular in the West. Many consumers have migrated to preferred provider organizations (PPOs), which blend the improved choice of traditional insurance with the affordability of HMOs. Under this plan, patients do not have to see a primary-care physician to get a referral to a specialist, and they can visit any doctor, though they enjoy considerable cost savings for using those within a PPO's network.

Ambulatory Services

The challenge of ambulatory services management also involves managing the needs of patients and many physicians and other providers working in the same physical facility. Many of these providers use the same resources, supplies, and laboratory, and they also share nursing and clinic nonprofessional staff. As is evident, this type of setting requires confident management and tact in dealing with people. Ambulatory managers often work in decentralized sites (freestanding) away from the parent organizations.

Behavioral Medicine and Mental Health

In 1956 Congress, with the urging of President Dwight D. Eisenhower, established the Joint Commission on Mental Illness in Health. It was this commission's final report that gave impetus to the growth of community mental-health services in this country. The report recommended an end to the construction of very large mental-health (psychiatric) hospitals and suggested that a flexible array of services be provided in the community for mental illness.

In 1963 Congress showed continued concern when it passed the Mental Retardation Facilities and Community Mental Health Centers Construction Act (Public Law 88-164). It was this act, and subsequent amendments to the act, that provided federal assistance to public and nonprofit facilities for the construction and staffing of community mental-health centers in this country. Today there are hundreds of such comprehensive centers in the United States.

The management of behavioral medicine activities is similar to the management of a hospital's ambulatory services. A mental-health administrator has to deal with many different types of professionals, including psychiatrists, psychologists, and social workers. There is heavy professional staffing in mental-health centers. Today's world of community mental-health centers seems to indicate that centers are moving toward an ever-increasing scope of professional resources with even larger and more diverse staffs. With such diverse staffs comes an increasingly complex organizational structure. This is a special challenge for the mental-health administrator. A mental-health administrator must be ready for close involvement with the government at all levels, as well as with the community in which the facility is located.

Long-Term-Care Institutions

Long-term care refers to physical- and mental-health services provided to temporarily or chronically disabled persons over an extended period of time, with a goal of enabling them to maintain as high as possible a level of independent functioning. The basic difference between long-term-care management and the administration of general hospitals rests in the nature of the patients' problems. In the long-term setting the institution's medical, nursing, and support services are all geared to patients whose physical and/or mental problems call for institutionalization over many months or even years.

Many management opportunities exist in the country's nursing homes. Today many health administration programs offer long-term-care concentrations at the master's degree level. Nursing homes are generally defined as the wide range of institutions that offer a variety of levels of care. Nursing homes include freestanding institutions that offer nursing service and related services from the skilled nursing facility to residential care.

Opportunities for management also can be found in related long-term institutional care, such as adult day care, hospice programs, and home health-care services. Home-health agencies provide health-care and supportive services to the disabled in their homes. The range of services offered by home health care is similar to that in the nursing home. For example, physical therapy, personal care, and homemaker's services are all available.

Insurance Companies

The insurance industry is also a valuable resource for those seeking a position in health-care management. The insurance industry works very closely with hospitals, nursing homes, and other institutions, as well as with doctors. The first health insurance plan in America started in 1929, when a group of schoolteachers in cooperation with Baylor Hospital in Dallas, Texas, made monthly payments in exchange for hospital coverage. From this seed grew the Blue Cross plans. Blue Cross plans were designed to cover hospital expenses, while Blue Shield plans were designed to cover doctor's visits. Today the Blue Cross and Blue Shield system is the nation's oldest and largest family of health benefits companies and comprises forty independent Blue plans.

The Blue Cross plans also offer numerous opportunities for the prospective health-care administrator. Blue Cross and Blue Shield plans cover ninety-three million people in the United States and also are involved in the Medicare-Medicaid programs as carriers under the doctor portion of that legislation. The graduate of a health administration program who goes into the public insurance field will quickly see how valuable public relations skills are in negotiating claims between companies and hospitals. The graduate will also value training in actuarial and rate-setting procedures.

Consultancies

The complex world of management and its other related administrative challenges of planning, association work, and insurance all require outside assistance of some nature from time to time. It is the health administrator as a consultant who meets this need. The consultant can bring a fresh approach or perspective to solving administrative problems. Consultants identify problems and recommend ways to solve them.

Consultants have been increasingly used at all levels in the health-care field and particularly by the government. Not only can a consultant bring a new perspective to a situation, but also his or her problem-solving proposals frequently prove to be the most cost-effective means of getting a difficult task accomplished. Since consultants are often requested to solve very technical problems, a graduate going into this field will need certain skills, such as a working knowledge of accounting, information systems, organization, and communications.

Other Health-Care Agencies

The federal government is the largest employer of health personnel in the country. Accordingly, there are many opportunities for health administration careers at a variety of governmental levels. Within the federal government, extensive programs that require trained health management professionals to administer them are operated by the Public Health Service and many other major governmental agencies such as the National Institutes of Health, Centers for Disease Control and Prevention, Health Resources and Services Administration, Health Services Administration, Food and Drug Administration, and Substance Abuse and Mental Health Services Administration. These agencies are in addition to the branches of the armed forces and the Department of Veterans Affairs, which maintain health programs as well as their own system of hospitals. The government offers a major segment of management employment to health-care administrators.

There are many opportunities in health planning for trained health administrators. For many recent graduates from health administration programs, health planning has provided an attractive alternative to institutional management levels, especially where hospitals in the same region have formed hospital councils.

7

Senior Care

There is a major change under way in our country. America has a population that is rapidly growing older. Never before has this country had so many older citizens. These older people face many challenges. Income, or lack of it, is often one of them. Retirement at sixty-five usually brings a reduction in income, yet the need for medical services tends to increase with advancing age. Inflationary pressures put a squeeze on older citizens. Living arrangements can also become a problem for the elderly. As people become older, especially beyond age sixty-five, the number of individuals living in a family unit decreases rapidly.

Another problem for the aged is their need for comprehensive health care and medical services. The acute medical care given by hospitals and skilled nursing homes is, for the most part, taken care of by the Medicare program, but other portions of care—particularly for the chronically and terminally ill—are not paid for adequately. The majority of the "most frail elderly" are over eighty-five years old. (See Table 7.1 and Table 7.2.)

Table 7.1 Distribution of U.S. Elderly Population by Age, 2000–2030

Age	2000 No.	% of Total Pop.	2010 (projected) No.	% of Total Pop.	2030 (projected) No.	% of Total Pop.
65+	34,991,753	12.4	40,243,713	12.9	71,453,471	19.5
65–69	9,533,545	3.4	12,172,070	3.9	19,980,262	5.5
70–74	8,857,441	3.1	9,097,439	2.9	17,967,671	4.9
75–79	7,415,813	2.6	7,186,229	2.3	13,988,906	3.8
80–84	4,945,367	1.8	5,664,517	1.8	9,913,598	2.7
85+	4,239,587	1.5	6,123,458	2.0	9,603,034	2.6

Source: U.S. Census Bureau, 2005.

Table 7.2 Distribution of Canadian Elderly Population by Age, 2001–2026

Age	2001 No. (in Millions)	% of Total Pop.	2011 (projected) No. (in Millions)	% of Total Pop.	2026 (projected) No. (in Millions)	% of Total Pop.
65+	3.88	13.0	4.81	14.8	7.75	21.4
65–69	1.13	3.8	1.49	4.6	2.40	6.6
70–79	1.82	6.1	1.99	6.1	3.48	9.6
80+	0.93	3.1	1.33	4.1	1.87	5.2

Adapted from Statistics Canada, CANSIM database: http://www12.statcan.ca/english/ census01/products/standard/themes/RetrieveProductTable.cfm? (2001 data); http://www 40.statcan.ca/101/cst01/demo23a.htm (2011 data); http://www40.statcan.ca/101/cst01/ demo23c.htm (2026 data).

Services and Institutions

There is a wide range of services and institutions available to meet the medical and personal needs of the elderly. (See Figure 7.1 and

Figure 7.1 Percentage of People 65 and Over with Moderate to Severe Memory Impairment

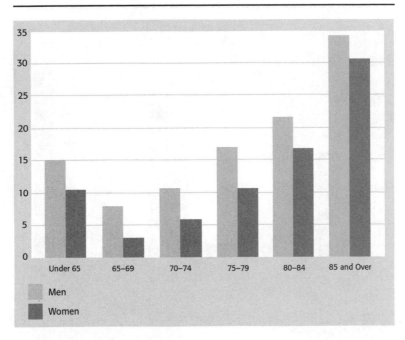

Source: Federal Interagency Forum on Aging-Related Statistics. *Older Americans 2004: Key Indicators of Well-Being.*

Figure 7.2.) This is a dynamic sector of the medical-care system that demands innovative planning and administration. Challenging administrative positions are available in this area.

Adult Day Health Center

An adult day health center, sometimes referred to as *adult day care*, serves both clients and their caregivers. Clients receive nursing/medical care and/or therapies and participate in stimulating social and

Figure 7.2 Percentage of Medicare Enrollees 65 and Over with Physical Limitations (Unable to . . .)

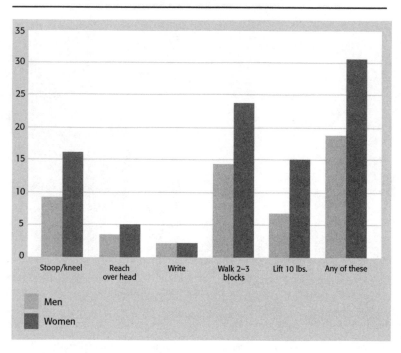

Source: Centers for Medicare and Medicaid Services, Medicare Current Beneficiary Survey.

recreational activities with peers. Caregivers receive the respite they need, along with education and counseling.

Alzheimer's (Dementia) Care Unit

The objectives of dementia care include the following.

1. To provide secure shelter, warmth, and food
2. To support any abilities not totally impaired by dementia

3. To ensure an appropriate range of environmental and sensory stimulation and information
4. To support and reinforce each resident's understanding of his or her place in time or space
5. To create unobtrusive opportunities for social interaction
6. To maintain an individual's right to privacy
7. To emphasize links with the past and the familiar in a homelike setting
8. To support programs that accommodate wandering in a safe environment
9. To define spaces into public, shared, semiprivate, private, and staff
10. To allow for future change and changing needs

Assisted-Living Facility

An assisted-living facility is a senior living complex that has physical features designed specifically to assist the frail elderly. It also has staff personnel and programs that help residents with the activities of daily living. Units might or might not have kitchens; however, meals are provided in a central location. Units usually rent on a monthly basis.

Comprehensive Outpatient Rehabilitation Facility

A comprehensive outpatient rehabilitation facility is a nonresidential facility that is established and operated exclusively for the purpose of providing diagnostic, therapeutic, and restorative services to outpatients. It is a single fixed location for the rehabilitation of injured, disabled, or sick persons who have either been sent there by a physician or are under the supervision of a physician.

Congregate-Care Facility

A congregate-care facility is a multifamily complex catering to seniors, primarily single women, which also has a common dining facility. Individual units have small kitchens for casual use. Limited support services such as linen service, housekeeping, transportation, and social activities may or may not be provided. Units also usually rent on a monthly basis.

Continuing-Care Retirement Community

A continuing-care retirement community (CCRC) is a senior living complex providing a continuum of care including housing, health care, and various support services. Health-care services such as nursing might be provided directly or through access to affiliated health-care facilities. Fees are structured as a refundable entry fee plus a monthly fee, as a condominium, as a rental, or as an endowment. The unit might require that the occupant maintain insurance.

The CCRC is also known as a life care center. Initially the term *life care center* became prevalent in the northeastern United States, while the term *continuing-care retirement community* was used widely in the western regions of the United States.

Home Health Care

Home health care is a coordinated program that provides medical care, nursing, and additional treatment and social services to patients in their place of residence.

Hospice/Hospice Care

Hospice care is a program providing palliative care—primarily medical relief of pain and symptoms management—and support services to terminally ill patients, as well as assistance to their families in adjusting to the patient's illness and death.

Hospital-Based Skilled Nursing Facility

A hospital-based skilled nursing facility provides medical and continuous nursing care services to nonacute patients who mainly require convalescent, rehabilitative, and/or restorative services. It may be located on or off the hospital campus, but it must meet the following three criteria:

1. Both the hospital and the nursing home must be governed by a common governing board.
2. Both the hospital and nursing home must file a common Medicare cost report.
3. The nursing home must obtain more than half of its services from the hospital.

Independent-Living Facilities

Independent-living facilities are multifamily complexes catering to active seniors, mostly couples, who are able to function independently. Support services, if offered, are hospitality related. Apartments might rent on a monthly basis or might have a condominium cooperative structure.

Intermediate Care

Intermediate-care services are health-related services provided to individuals who do not require hospital or skilled nursing care, but whose condition requires services that are above the level of room and board and can be made available only in an inpatient setting.

Membership Packages for Seniors

There are membership packages for seniors whereby hospitals or other provider organizations offer extra benefits to older consumers who join such programs. Seniors are offered a wide range of benefits, including assistance in filling out Medicare and insurance forms, discounts on drugs and on meals in the hospital cafeterias, and referrals to physicians who will not charge patients beyond what Medicare pays.

Nursing Homes

Nursing homes are extended-care facilities. *Nursing home* is a broad term that includes several levels of care and types of programs. The two levels of care that are most commonly associated with nursing homes are the skilled nursing-care facility and the intermediate-care facility.

Personal-Care Facilities

Personal-care facilities are living arrangements that provide residents with meals as well as assistance with bathing, dressing, toileting, and other activities of daily living. With certain exceptions, nursing care is not provided. These might also be referred to as *boarding home*s.

Telephone Contact/Helpline

A telephone contact/helpline service might provide one or all of the following: counseling, information, referral, and check-up services or monitoring of all health-related problems.

Transportation Services

Transportation services provide or arrange for transportation to allow disabled or older adults to meet daily needs and to have access to a broad range of services.

Wellness Programs

Wellness programs include health maintenance, disease prevention, and exercise programs for social, psychological, and physical well-being. Examples include risk reduction (such as smoking-cessation and weight-reduction programs), education in health and nutrition, and exercise and stress-management programs.

Long-Term-Care Administrator

The long-term-care administrator should have the basic characteristics of any successful manager: skills in planning, organizing, diplomacy, and leadership. Expertise in finance and health-care organizations is also important. But in addition to these traits, the long-term-care administrator has to adapt to the unique aspects of this part of the medical-care system and possess the following:

• **An understanding of the concept of comprehensive health.** In working with geriatric centers, an administrator has a major coordinating role. He or she must help develop programs for patient placement and discharge as appropriate.

• **An understanding of the needs of the aged and chronically ill and the know-how to provide for those needs.** Understanding the causes and reasons for chronic illness is the first step in providing an effective program and environment.

• **The knowledge that teaching in this environment is important.** Working with the aged and chronically ill can be depressing and frustrating. The administrator must be able to establish educational programs to sensitize staff members to the special problems and opportunities in this area.

• **A desire to be an agent of change.** Long-term care is a changing field. There are many opportunities for innovation. The administrator must be bold enough to seek change.

Motivated and well-trained long-term-care administrators are always in demand. The range of choices in types of care and the number of institutions continue to grow. If you have the personality for this special administrative work and the ambition to study and grow, long-term-care administration could be in your managerial future.

8

Educational Preparation

An effective health administrator performs basic management functions such as assisting with policy follow-through, managing personnel and materials, and establishing and monitoring budgets. Most administrators are also involved in public relations activities.

In days past, administrators were frequently secured from other professional ranks. In fact, many administrators were former nursing administrators, physicians, and accountants. Yet because of the variety of activities and departments an administrator is responsible for today, a specialized educational background is now required for the job. In 2005 the American College of Healthcare Executives reported that 86 percent of its members had a master's degree or higher, and of those who held a master's, more than two-thirds majored in hospital/health services administration, public health/public administration, or clinical/allied health administration. Twenty-five percent of its member executives with master's degrees majored in business.

Formal Training

Health care is a very dynamic field, and it requires early preparation and continuing education throughout an administrator's career.
Dozens of schools now offer degree programs aimed at those students wishing to go into hospital and health-care administration.
Appendixes A and B list contact information for graduate and
undergraduate degree programs in the United States, Canada, and
Puerto Rico. Some of these programs are located in schools of business. Other programs are in schools of public health or in selected
interdisciplinary settings.

The master's degree is most widely accepted as the required academic preparation for health administration. Many of these programs offer full- and part-time study so that students can both work
in their current positions and continue to grow professionally by
attending school.

Many of the master's degree programs have as part of their curriculum some type of an internship or residency. During this time
students in the master's degree program go into a health-care organization for a period of many weeks or months to learn and work.
A much briefer period may be called a *clerkship*. During residency,
students spending time in hospitals rotate through various departments of the hospital. Many students go directly from undergraduate school into the master's degree program; however, schools do
still look with favor on individuals who have had practical experience in the health-care field.

Many master's programs are based in a business administration
school, and they offer a master of business administration degree
(M.B.A.) with a concentration in health administration. Some programs offer the master of public administration (M.P.A.); others
base their program in health-care administration in the public
health school and offer a master of public health. Still other pro-

grams offer a master of science in health administration, and some a master in hospital administration. (See Table 8.1.)

Graduate Curriculum Programs

University graduate education involves two areas: the fundamental management/administrative course work; and practical, hands-on experience such as management research projects and clerkships. This also includes the residency.

Table 8.1 Active Members of the American College of Healthcare Executives by Educational Degree, Major, and Age*

Education		
Doctorate or two master's	5,208	18.2%
One master's	19,373	67.6%
Bachelor's or less	4,077	14.2%
Master's Degree Major		
Hospital/health services administration	14,100	58.7%
Business	5,510	23.0%
Public health/public administration	708	2.9%
Clinical/allied health administration	2,014	8.4%
Other	1,672	7.0%
Age		
< 30	2,373	8.7%
30–39	5,373	19.7%
40–49	8,074	29.5%
50–59	9,452	34.6%
60+	2,068	7.6%

* Statistics do not include student members or those of other special status.

Source: American College of Healthcare Executives, ACHE Affiliate Profile: 2006. www.ache.org.

The course work is focused mainly on management skill requirements relevant to the health industry such as personnel management, organization behavior, quantitative methods, law, finance,
information systems, strategic planning, policy development, marketing, and labor relations. Knowledge of social, ethical, political,
economic, and legal forces that influence the development of organizations is necessary for successful performance in this field. An
understanding of areas such as social and behavioral disciplines;
individual, social, and environmental health; and disease control is
also desirable.

As a general rule, graduate programs in health administration
cover three principal learning areas. One area covered in most programs is management theory. This includes traditional management
principles as well as health-care administrative theory and organization. This area also covers financial management, economics,
human relations, and the behavioral sciences.

The second learning area covered in most programs deals with
the health- and medical-care system. Included in this topic is a
detailed explanation of health-care organizations and their various
functions. Also covered are the issues that affect the system, including environmental and personal health characteristics, among others. Planning and economic considerations in the health-care system
are also covered.

Third are programs that cover more specific issues related to hospitals and health institutions. In this area the roles of health-care
institutions and providers within the health-care system are exam-
ined. Also, the specifics of managing health-care finances, personnel, and resources are covered, including study of the medical staff
and quality care issues.

No matter in which school a graduate program is offered, most
require the equivalent of at least two full years of study. Some

schools will offer certain types of fieldwork in addition to or as part of the two years of study. This is usually known as an *administrative residency*, and it is conducted under the supervision of a practicing administrator.

Undergraduate Programs

Undergraduate programs came of age in the early 1970s. In addition to preparing students for institutions that are less complex than hospitals—nursing homes, clinics, and group practices, for example—they serve as an early health-care track for those who wish to earn master's degrees in the field. There is a wide variety of undergraduate programs available, but they generally offer students three options.

1. General administration
2. Specialist training in a specific discipline such as financial management
3. A focus on a specific segment of the industry such as ambulatory care or long-term care

The Association of University Programs in Health Administration certifies undergraduate programs in the United States and Canada and maintains a list online at www.aupha.org (click on "Academic Member Programs").

Selecting an Educational Program

Students should research a variety of schools before finally selecting one. If they do, they will be faced with comparing perhaps several different programs. Which program is best for you, and how do you go about determining this? There are a variety of factors to consider, including the following.

- Tuition and other costs in the program
- Class size and the ratio of faculty to students
- Percentage of full-time versus part-time faculty
- Amount of research and publishing done by the faculty
- Core curriculum—business, public administration, or public health
- The program's job-placement service
- Length of time for field experience (clerkships, internships, and residencies)

A license is not required to work in health-care administration. This is not true in every administrative area, however. For example, all states and the District of Columbia require nursing-home administrators to be licensed; yet licensing might not be directly related to a master's degree program. Generally the states, though not uniformly, require a specified level of education, such as a bachelor's degree, plus some experience in the field.

Postgraduate Training and Continuing Education

Postgraduate training can include specific fellowship programs, which usually last one to two years and serve as a structured transition between the academic setting and full-time independent employment, as well as management development programs, which are fluid, usually short-term forms of continuing education. Fellowships provide practical experience in a health-care setting after receiving a master's degree. Some health-care settings include university teaching hospital/medical schools, hospitals, managed-care organizations, insurance companies, multi-institutional organizations, foundations, and associations. A list of fellowship opportunities is available on the American College of Healthcare Executives' website, called the "Directory of Fellowships in Health Services Administration" (www.ache.org/pgfd). This is an up-to-date list of postgraduate fellowships and management programs in the United States. *Management development program* is a more general term that applies to everything from online weekend seminars to real-world conferences and the curricula of corporate universities focused on advancing management skills in health care.

Learning is a lifelong experience. The professional administrator should not be satisfied with having earned an undergraduate or graduate degree. It is incumbent upon modern health-care managers to continue their education through formal continuing education programs. The American College of Healthcare Executives offers some of the very finest comprehensive continuing educational opportunities and professional development programs for its members. Its programs include seminars on problem-solving, on the development of management skills, and on a variety of other pertinent subjects essential for the dedicated health-care manager. As in so many professions, it is important for top people in the field to stay up to date on contemporary developments. Individuals going into health administration must be prepared to continue to keep current by reading regularly the professional periodicals and journals that are available through the American College of Healthcare Executives and other professional associations. A list of professional associations and selected journals is provided in Appendix C.

The master's degree continues to be the most widely recognized means of preparing for a career in health administration. This is because of the success over the past decades of the men and women who, holding master's degrees, have accomplished so much in the management of health-care institutions and systems. Because the field is changing and rapidly expanding, there will continue to be a demand for well-trained administrators.

9

GETTING THE JOB

WHEN YOU DECIDE that it's time to seek a position in health administration, remember that you not only will be competing against your peers—you will also be competing against yourself. The more you do to advance your job-hunting skills now, the better equipped you will be to face the challenge of the future. Two channels exist for job searches: published sources and unpublished sources. First let's discuss the method that is used most often.

Statistics prove that three-fourths of all job candidates in the health administration market secure their positions through personal contacts. Offhand you may be thinking that you are a member of the remaining quarter of applicants who must use other innovative measures to locate a job. This is not necessarily so. If you examine your own personal contacts (referred to as your *network*) you may be surprised to learn how many of them can be influential to your benefit.

Networking

Draw up a network identification form by creating four columns on a piece of paper and listing on it the following main headings (one in each column): "professional colleagues," "academic associations," "friends and acquaintances," and "relatives." Systematically fill in the columns with names of people who might be able to help you, no matter how remote the chances seem at present. You may be surprised at the number of people with power who are at your fingertips. Do not hesitate to ask those contacts to help guide you in your employment search. Remember, it means a great deal to speak directly with hospital administrators, assistant administrators, personnel directors, public relations directors, or any influential member of the hospital or institution you might want to join. Such people may be in your network.

Several other job sources are available to you, as well. Let's take a look at the remaining 25 percent of the jobs given to job searchers every year. These jobs are obtained usually through published sources. Comprehensive online job search sites such as Monster (www.monster.com) and HotJobs (www.hotjobs.com) will give you a good idea of the opportunities available, where demand lies, and what employers expect. The Web can also steer you to health-care-specific job sites such as HealthJobsUSA (www.healthjobsusa.com) and HealthCare Job Bank (www.healthcarejobbank .com). In addition, many of the graduate programs in hospital administration have alumni bulletins that have handy references to job sources. Try to get in touch with these associations and obtain these publications. You could also use your state and local health-care associations. Frequently they know about jobs.

Newspapers represent yet another good source. Looking at these sources is a routine you should get into. Without a doubt, however, the Sunday *New York Times* and the *Wall Street Journal* are two excellent newspapers that carry health-care administration openings. Some other sources, especially professional journals, that you should review regularly include: *Hospitals & Health Networks, Modern Healthcare, Healthcare Financial Management,* and the *American Journal of Public Health.* Refer to Appendix C of this book for a selected list of the health-care journals that often carry job listings.

Preparing Your Résumé

Chances are your résumé will introduce you to your prospective employer. Because this first impression is so important, let us spend some time showing you how to present yourself attractively on paper. It is up to you to tell the prospective employer why he or she should hire you based on the following information: who you are, what you know, what you have done, and what you would like to do for the new employer. When creating your résumé, keep in mind that you must be able to support its contents. You may be requested to exemplify your statements during a personal interview. Should this occur, you would be expected to add details without hesitation. Failure to do so could cost you the interview and the job.

The two most popular résumé styles used by people in health administration are the functional and the accomplishment résumés. Both contain the standard autobiographical data, such as your name, address, telephone number, education history, and work experiences. But they differ in their approach to employment description.

The functional résumé can be advantageous to people with considerable field experience or to those who are just embarking upon the health-care area after being employed in another field for a number of years. The functional résumé features specific jobs a person has held with minimal supplemental information about accomplishments in that job. For example, you might find the following entry in a functional résumé:

2003 to present
Community Hospital, Charlottesville, NC
Assistant controller in 200-bed hospital. Reported directly to the controller. Responsible for supervision of 17 people and a budget of $1.4 million.

However, in contrast to the functional résumé, the accomplishment résumé places considerable emphasis upon the applicant's achievements. A typical entry in an accomplishment résumé might include the following:

2005 to present
Assistant Financial Manager
Reorganized a department of 15 people with the result of increasing productivity by 40% and decreasing cost by 15%.

This type of résumé is more interesting to the employer because actual achievements are listed. By listing your accomplishments in specifics, you clearly spell out what you have done in the past and indicate what you are capable of achieving in the future.

Let's review some of the basic guidelines for developing an effective résumé that are listed in the following "dos" and "don'ts."

Dos of Preparing a Résumé
Start a permanent résumé file.
List all your education, experience, and achievements.
Know the kind of work you are seeking.
Be sure to place your name, address, and telephone number
   at the top of the résumé.
Give personal information at the end of the résumé.

Be specific.
Be quantitative.
Use action words.
Keep it short (one or two pages).
Use good bond, white or off-white paper.
Write a cover letter on the same bond paper.
Check and recheck for typing errors and misspellings.

Don'ts of Preparing a Résumé
Don't include job requirements.
Don't discuss lack of employment.
Don't discuss reasons for leaving your present job.
Don't use gimmicks.
Don't criticize your former employers.
Don't include a photograph of yourself.
Don't use the word "I."
Don't use abbreviations.

The Cover Letter

Every time you send a résumé to a potential employer, you must include a cover letter. Often it is this letter that determines whether you will be granted an interview. The cover letter must be tailored so you will have the competitive edge over other applicants. If you have trouble writing letters, get someone who can write persuasively to aid you in this undertaking.

Let us suppose that you have applied for a position as an administrative assistant at a local hospital. About a hundred other people have also applied. Somehow you have to stand apart from the crowd at the outset. You have to grab the employer's attention by using a degree of flair. Your cover letter introduces you to the employer and hopefully arrests his or her attention, stimulates interest in you, and convinces the employer that you are the person he or she most wants to interview.

Let's spend some time reviewing the basic elements of a cover letter. First make sure that your name, complete address, home and cell phone numbers with area code, and the date are in the upper right-hand corner of your cover letter. If you are employed, include your business office telephone for initial contact. However, you might want to list a special time when you can be reached elsewhere. The idea is to make it as easy as possible for the employer to contact you. When an employer can choose from more than a hundred applications for the same job, it is doubtful that much time will be spent trying to figure out a way to reach a potential candidate.

Next, address the person to whom you are writing by name, if possible. Sometimes you will know the person's name, and other times it will not be listed in the ad. Therefore, you may have to use your network if you are to write a personal letter. You could also call the hospital or the organization and request the name of the personnel director or the administrator. Remember, you must gain a favorable impression from the start.

What should you include in the body of the cover letter? This depends on why you are writing a letter in the first place. For example, if you were referred by a friend or a colleague from your network, you could be writing an unsolicited letter that announces your availability, or you could be answering a publicized job opening. No matter what your reason is, the first thing you must do is establish for the reader exactly why you are writing. In the first sentence you might want to say something like, "I am writing you in response to your advertisement for an administrative assistant that was published in the *Philadelphia Inquirer*, July 14."

Successful Interviewing

By now you should be ready for the climax of your job campaign—the interview. You have already realistically assessed your goals, utilizing the network; designed an attractive résumé; and written a dynamic cover letter.

If your interview experience is limited or nonexistent, you are probably uncertain or hesitant about what to say or how to say it. To gain practice, you can participate in role-playing exercises. Ask a friend to engage in a mock interview session with you.

Most interviewers use a question-and-answer format. Your task is to respond quickly and intelligently. Chances are you will be asked a few personal questions to break the ice. It is safe to assume you will be asked some of the following questions:

- What do you know about our hospital or institution?
- What can I do for you?
- What do you consider your strongest management skill?
- Why do you want to join our staff?
- What will you be doing in five years? Ten years?
- What can you tell me about yourself?

If you are being interviewed on a one-to-one basis, you will have to handle some things differently than if you are interviewed before a group. As the administrator or the personnel director talks to you, be sure to take notes. Most administrators and interviewers feel that note taking signifies an organized, interested applicant.

Now let's review some of the important elements in handling the interview:

- Practice beforehand.
- Be yourself, not an actor.
- Bring extra copies of your résumé.
- Study your résumé beforehand.
- Tell the interviewers what you can do for them.
- Know and be prepared to discuss three or four of your strongest assets.
- Don't end on a flat negative.
- Don't waste precious time discussing your hobbies.
- Be specific and to the point.
- Keep to the facts; minimize opinions.
- Never argue with the interviewer.
- Be a good listener.
- Take notes.

Follow-Up and Accepting the Job

The first thing you want to do when you leave the interview, whether it was with the administrator or the personnel director, is review the notes you took. Even though you may not have been able to jot down everything you wanted to, take the time now to add any important notes you omitted earlier. For example, if the administrator confided in you that he or she is having a terrible time trying to find a director of nurses who will produce dynamic results, make sure you not only include this tip, but also underline it for emphasis. You can capitalize on the situation. Note taking is very important.

You may not always be told why you were rejected by an employer. If this happens, you should contact the administrator or personnel director and ask why you are no longer in the running. While this may seem like a painful procedure, you need to make every effort to find out exactly what the reasons were for your elimination. What if you lost the job because of insufficient technical knowledge? If you do not find this out at the start of your job campaign, you can be destroyed in interview after interview. You must be able to correct this gap in your knowledge.

Doing Well in Your First Job

Once you have been selected for a position and have negotiated a fair salary, it is time to start work. Now the question is, how do you make a success of your job in health administration? Success is not just getting your position—it is doing well in that position and eventually getting promoted.

There are several things that working administrators should do if they want to be successful. The manager should strive to build a results-oriented track record. This may be the most important advice to the novice manager. Take your job seriously, attack projects with hard work and imagination, and get results.

Administrators must continually develop their communication, public relations, and quantitative skills. By consistently working on your weak areas, you upgrade your competency as an administrator. Administrators must continue their training and development even after their formal schooling. Setting aside time to read professional journals and attending educational seminars and conferences are excellent ways to keep up to date and to improve your job skills.

You should know the formal process of how you will be evaluated on the job and specifically what criteria will be used. As a manager, you should know what your boss expects of you. Remember there is also an informal process of performance review. Do not count only on the formal system—be a top-notch performer at all times. You should ask your boss for feedback on your performance. It is your obligation to ask for it—and your boss's obligation to give you a review of your performance.

Try to be a likeable person and set up alliances among your managerial peers. This is very much a part of establishing a job network that will assist you in future promotions. Managers should recognize the two "A" principles—ability and affability. There is no sense in creating ill will in your job. Respect for fellow employees is important.

If you do well in your job, you will undoubtedly be very busy. Administrators must learn to delegate. By delegating, you will also be developing your responsibility to others. This is important for your own development, too. There may come a time that your boss will consider promoting you. One consideration will be who, in turn, is capable of taking your position. Therefore, training an adequate replacement may allow you to be promoted within the same institution. A competent assistant will also permit you to leave your job from time to time to attend educational programs or industry events. If you achieve results and are a top-notch performer, the time will come to move up to a position of greater responsibility. If the new job is in another institution, you should leave your present position under the best of circumstances. Don't "muddy the waters" just because you have a new job. Leave with good relations and on your own timetable.

The Outlook for Jobs

Because health care is changing so rapidly and the challenges in the industry are significant, the job outlook for new entrants to the field is promising. The administrators of today's hospitals and care facilities will stake their futures on the ingenuity and discipline of the bright young minds entering their ranks. An ability to change quickly, continually adjust perceptions and priorities, and apply new resources to existing problems will mark workers who find success.

Those who can speak Spanish as well as English will have greater opportunity and more flexibility in where they work. Tomorrow's administrators also are more likely to find themselves working for larger organizations with decentralized facilities that stay connected with high-tech communications technology. Those who understand what the technology can do for them and how to manage it properly will be at a distinct advantage.

Financial constraints will continue to be the number-one challenge for hospitals and care facilities, far above issues such as quality and patient satisfaction. The environment is just as pressing for these institutions as it is for consumers of health care. Financial acumen and sound business decisions will be more important than ever.

Diversity in Health Administration

The industry is hungry for ethnic diversity. African-Americans and Hispanics are underrepresented in health-care administration as well as the health-care field at large. While the two groups along with American Indians comprise about 25 percent of the population, they account for only about 8 percent of health-care executives.

Breakdown by gender is less dramatic, with women representing about 40 percent of health-care executives. (See Table 9.1.)

America's population at large will be diverse and dynamic throughout the twenty-first century, and the health-care labor force that serves it must be also. Minorities can expect to see the door swing open progressively wider when it comes to securing positions in the field, a trend that will serve patients and administrators equally well.

Table 9.1 Distribution of ACHE Members by Race and Gender

Gender

Female	11,717	40.7%
Male	17,082	59.3%

Race

White, not Hispanic	15,480	88.8%
Black	929	5.3%
Hispanic	486	2.8%
Asian, Pacific	460	2.6%
American Indian/Alaskan	83	0.5%

Source: American College of Healthcare Executives, ACHE Affiliate Profile: 2006. www.ache.org.

APPENDIX A

Graduate Programs in Health Services Administration

THE SCHOOLS LISTED below offer graduate programs in health services administration that are accredited by the Commission on Accreditation of Healthcare Management Education.*

Arizona State University
School of Health Management and Policy
M.B.A./M.H.S.M. Dual-Degree Program
Evening M.H.S.M. Program
http://wpcarey.asu.edu/hap

Army-Baylor University
Graduate Program in Healthcare Administration
www.cs.amedd.army.mil/baylorhca/default1.htm

---

* Source: *Healthcare Management Education 2005–2007 Directory of Programs*, The Association of University Programs in Health Administration (AUPHA).

Baruch College/City University of New York
Baruch/Mt. Sinai Graduate Program
www.healthcaremba.org

Boston University
Health Care Management Program
http://management.bu.edu/gpo/hc/index.asp

California State University–Long Beach
Health Care Administration Program
www.csulb.edu/depts/hca

Cleveland State University
Graduate Study in Health Care Administration
www.csuohio.edu/hca

Cornell University
Sloan Program in Health Administration
www.sloan.cornell.edu

Dalhousie University
School of Health Services Administration
www.dal.ca/shsa

Duke University
Health Sector Management Program
www.fuqua.duke.edu/programs/hsm

Florida International University
Program in Health Policy and Management
http://chua2.fiu.edu/hsa

George Washington University
Department of Health Services Management and Leadership
www.gwumc.edu/sphhs/hsml/index.html

Georgia State University
Institute of Health Administration
Robinson School of Business
http://robinson.gsu.edu

Governors State University
Department of Health Administration
www.govst.edu/chp/mha

Graduate College at Union University
Program in Health Systems Administration
www.gcuu.edu/pages/schools/management/degreepro2.asp

Indiana University
Graduate Program in Health Administration
www.mha.iupui.edu

Johns Hopkins University
Department of Health Policy and Management
Master of Health Science in Health Finance and Management
www.jhsph.edu/dept/hpm

King's College
Master of Science in Health Care Administration
http://departments.kings.edu/graduate/prog_req.html#3

Marymount University
Master of Science, Health Promotion Management
School of Business Administration
www.marymount.edu/academic/healthprof/hhp/
   programs.html#hpm

Medical University of South Carolina
Master of Health Administration Program
www.musc.edu

New York University
Master of Public Administration in Health Policy and Management
www.wagner.nyu.edu

Northwestern University
Program in Health Industry Management
Kellogg Graduate School of Management
www.kellogg.northwestern.edu/academic/health/index.htm

Ohio State University
Division of Health Services Management and Policy
http://sph.osu.edu/hsmp

Pennsylvania State University
Master of Health Administration
Department of Health Policy and Administration
www.hhdev.psu.edu/hpa

Rush University
Master of Science in Health Systems Management
www.rushu.rush.edu/hsm

Saint Louis University
Department of Health Management and Policy
http://publichealth.slu.edu/programs/mha/Default.htm

San Diego State University
Division of Health Services Administration
http://publichealth.sdsu.edu

Simmons College
Graduate Program in Health Care Administration
www.simmons.edu/shs/academics/hca

Temple University
Department of Risk
Insurance and Healthcare Management
www.sbm.temple.edu/~hadept

Texas State University–San Marcos
Graduate Program in Healthcare Administration
www.health.txstate.edu/ha

Texas Tech University
M.B.A. and M.D./M.B.A. Program in Health Organization
   Management
www.hom.ba.ttu.edu

Texas Woman's University–Houston
Houston Center Program in Health Care Administration
www.twu.edu/hs/h-hca

Trinity University
Graduate Program in Health Care Administration
www.trinity.edu/departments/healthcare

Tulane University
Department of Health Systems Management
www.hsm.tulane.edu

University of Alabama at Birmingham
Department of Health Services Administration
M.S.H.A. Program
www.uab.edu/hsa

University of Arkansas–Little Rock
Graduate Program in Health Services Administration
www.ualr.edu/hsadmin

University of California–Berkeley
Graduate Program in Health Management
www.haas.berkeley.edu/advantage/health.htm

University of California–Los Angeles
Health Policy and Management Program
www.ph.ucla.edu/hs

University of Central Florida
Health Services Administration Program
www.cohpa.ucf.edu/health.pro/hsams.cfm

University of Colorado at Denver
Programs in Health Services Administration
www.cudenver.edu/business

University of Florida
Department of Health Services Research, Management, and Policy
www.phhp.ufl.edu/hsrmp

University of Houston–Clear Lake
Healthcare Administration Program
www.cl.uh.edu/bpa/hadm

University of Iowa
Department of Health Management and Policy
www.public-health.uiowa.edu/hmp

University of Kansas Medical Center
Department of Health Policy and Management
www.kumc.edu/som/hpm

University of Kentucky
Master of Health Administration Program
www-martin.uky.edu/~web/programs/mha/mha.html

University of Memphis
Division of Health Administration
http://healthadmin.memphis.edu

University of Miami
Health Administration and Policy Program
www.bus.miami.edu/grad

University of Michigan
Master of Health Management and Policy
School of Public Health
www.sph.umich.edu/hmp

University of Minnesota–Twin Cities
Program in Healthcare Administration
www.carlsonschool.umn.edu/mha

University of Missouri–Columbia
Health Services Management
www.hmi.missouri.edu

Université de Montréal
Master's Program in Health Services Administration
www.mdas.umontreal.ca

University of North Carolina–Chapel Hill
Department of Health Policy and Administration
www.sph.unc.edu/hpaa

University of Oklahoma
Department of Health Administration and Policy
http://w3.ouhsc.edu/hap

University of Pennsylvania
Graduate Program in Health Care Management
www.wharton.upenn.edu

University of Pittsburgh
Health Administration Program
www.hpm.pitt.edu

University of Puerto Rico
Master in Health Services Administration
Graduate School of Public Health
www.rcm.upr.edu/publichealth/english/index_e.html

University of Saint Thomas
M.B.A. in Medical Group Management
www.stthomas.edu/mmgm

University of Scranton
Graduate Program in Health Administration
http://academic.uofs.edu/department/hahr/mha

University of South Carolina
Master of Health Administration Program
http://hspm.sph.sc.edu

University of Southern California
Health Management and Policy Program
www.usc.edu/schools/sppd

University of Southern Maine
Graduate Program in Health Policy and Management
http://muskie.usm.maine.edu/academics/acad_hpm.jsp

University of Toronto
Graduate Department of Health Policy, Management, and
    Evaluation
www.hpme.utoronto.ca/scripts/index_.asp

University of Washington–Seattle
Graduate Programs in Health Services Administration
http://depts.washington.edu/mhap

Virginia Commonwealth University
Graduate Program in Health Administration
www.had.vcu.edu

Washington State University at Spokane
Graduate Program in Health Policy and Administration
www.hpa.spokane.wsu.edu

Washington University–St. Louis
Health Administration Program
http://hap.wustl.edu

Widener University
Graduate Program in Health and Medical Services Administration
www.sba.widener.edu

Xavier University
Graduate Program in Health Services Administration
www.xavier.edu/mhsa

Yale University
Health Management Program
http://info.med.yale.edu/eph/html/divisions/hpa/hmp.html

Undergraduate Programs in Health Services Administration

THE SCHOOLS LISTED below offer undergraduate programs in health services administration that are accredited by the Commission on Accreditation of Healthcare Management Education.*

Appalachian State University
Health Care Management Program
www.business.appstate.edu/departments/management/hcm

Auburn University
Health Administration Program
www.auburn.edu/ha

---

* Source: *Healthcare Management Education 2005–2007 Directory of Programs*, The Association of University Programs in Health Administration (AUPHA).

California State University–Chico
Health Services Administration Program
www.csuchico.edu/hcsv

California State University–Long Beach
Health Care Administration Program
www.csulb.edu/depts/hca

California State University–Northridge
Health Administration Program
http://hhd.csun.edu/hsci

Clayton College and State University
Department of Health Care Management
http://healthsci.clayton.edu/hsprogshcm.htm

Florida A & M University
Division of Health Care Management
www.famu.edu/acad/colleges/ahs/hcm.cfm

Governors State University
College of Health Professions
www.govst.edu/ha

Howard University
Health Management Sciences Program
www.cpnahs.howard.edu/ahs/programs.htm

Idaho State University
Health Care Administration Department
www.isu.edu/departments/hcadmin

James Madison University
Health Services Administration Program
www.healthsci.jmu.edu/hsa/pages

Mary Baldwin College
Health Care Administration Program
www.mbc.edu/academic/departments/hca.asp

Metropolitan State College at Denver
Health Care Management Program
www.mscd.edu/~hep

Oregon State University
Department of Public Health
www.hhs.oregonstate.edu/ph/undergrad/index.html

Pennsylvania State University
Baccalaureate Program, Department of Health
    Policy and Administration
www.hhdev.psu.edu/hpa

Richard Stockton College of New Jersey
Division of Professional Studies
http://aden.stockton.edu/cgi-bin/ug-program-list?program=pubh

Ryerson University
Health Services Management Program
www.ryerson.ca/~hsm

Slippery Rock University
School of Business
www.sru.edu/pages/1528.asp

State University of New York Institute of Technology
Health Service Management Programs
http://people.sunyit.edu/~fgds

Stonehill College
Department of Health Care Administration
www.stonehill.edu/hca

Tennessee State University
Health Administration and Health Sciences
www.tnstate.edu/interior.asp?ptid=1&mid=1133

Texas State University–San Marcos
Baccalaureate Program in Healthcare Administration
www.health.txstate.edu/ha

Towson University
Health Care Management Program
www.towson.edu/hcmn

University of Alabama at Tuscaloosa
Health Care Management
http://management.cba.ua.edu/hcm

University of Connecticut
Center for Healthcare and Insurance Studies
www.business.uconn.edu/healthcare

University of Michigan–Flint
Department of Health Sciences and Administration
www.umflint.edu/hcr

University of Nevada–Las Vegas
Health Care Administration Program
http://hca.unlv.edu

University of New Hampshire
Department of Health Management and Policy
www.unh.edu/hmp

University of North Carolina–Chapel Hill
Department of Health Policy and Administration
www.sph.unc.edu/hpaa

University of North Florida
Health Administration Programs
www.unf.edu/coh/bshadm.htm

University of Scranton
Undergraduate Health Administration Program
http://matrix.scranton.edu/academics/ac_pgm_health
  _administration.shtml

University of South Dakota
Health Services Administration Division
www.usd.edu/business/hsad/home.cfm

University of Wisconsin–Milwaukee
Health Care Administration and Informatics Program
http://cfprod.imt.uwm.edu/chs/academics/undergraduate/
  healthsciences/healthcare

Weber State University
Health Administration Services Program
www.weber.edu/has

Western Kentucky University
Health Care Administration Programs
www.wku.edu/health

Appendix C
Professional Societies and Selected Journals

Professional Society Membership

American Academy of Medical Administrators
701 Lee St., Ste. 600
Des Plaines, IL 60016
www.aameda.org

The American Academy of Medical Administrators (AAMA) was founded in Boston in 1957 and today has a membership of more than three thousand health-care professionals in the United States, Canada, the Caribbean, and elsewhere. The mission of the AAMA, a not-for-profit association of health-care professionals, is to develop and refine concepts and practices in the field of health-care administration and to promote the advancement of its members in knowledge, professional development, credentialing, and personal achievements through continuing education and research in health-care management.

The AAMA has developed new and innovative approaches in fulfilling its commitment to all levels of management within health administration through the founding of new chapter organizations. The academy has formed these organizations to assist professional managers in special areas such as cardiology, oncology, information systems, home health, and neuromusculoskeletal areas.

American College of Health Care Administrators
300 N. Lee St., Ste. 301
Alexandria, VA 22314
www.achca.org

The American College of Health Care Administrators (ACHCA) is a professional society of administrators of long-term health programs serving the aged and chronically ill. Founded in 1962 as the American College of Nursing Home Administrators, ACHCA is the only organization representing the professional long-term-care administrator.

ACHCA is dedicated to the professional advancement of the long-term-care health administrator through education, research, informational services, professional representation, and leadership.

American College of Healthcare Executives
1 N. Franklin St., Ste. 1700
Chicago, IL 60606
www.ache.org

The American College of Healthcare Executives (ACHE) is an international professional society of thirty thousand health-care executives. The college is known for its prestigious credentialing and educational programs. ACHE's annual Congress on Healthcare Management draws more than four thousand participants each year. The college is also known for its journal, *Journal of Healthcare Management*, and its magazine, *Healthcare Executive*, as well as groundbreaking research and career development and public policy programs. Through such efforts, the college works toward its goal of improving the health status of society by advancing health-care management excellence.

American College of Physician Executives
4890 W. Kennedy Blvd., Ste. 200
Tampa, FL 33609
www.acpe.org

The American College of Physician Executives (ACPE), formerly the American Academy of Medical Directors, was founded in 1975 and is a national, professional, and educational association exclusively for physicians in positions of organizational leadership throughout the United States.

The ACPE is recognized by the American Medical Association as the national specialty society representing medical management. It currently serves more than nine thousand physicians who hold positions of medical director, chief executive officer, vice president of medical affairs, dean, chief of staff, and chief of service in hospitals, group practices, managed-care organizations, universities, industry, insurance, and government.

American Public Health Association
800 I St. NW
Washington, DC 20001
www.apha.org

Established in 1872, the American Public Health Association (APHA) is devoted to the universal protection and promotion of public health and the equality of health services for all persons.

The APHA achieves these goals by (1) setting standards for alleviating health problems, (2) initiating projects designed for improving health both nationally and internationally, (3) researching health problems and offering solutions based on that research, (4) launching public awareness campaigns about specific health dangers, (5) publishing numerous materials reflecting the latest findings and developments in public health, and (6) publicizing a year-round schedule of action implementation programs. Throughout its history, APHA has fostered significant advancement in personal health services; improved the environment, training, and credentialing of health professionals; and worked for the prevention of disease.

The membership represents all of the disciplines and specialties in public health. Twenty-four special sections represent the various disciplines and special interest areas within APHA.

Association of Behavioral Healthcare Management

12300 Twinbrook Pkwy., Ste. 320
Rockville, MD 20852
www.nccbh.org/abhm

Now a section of the National Council for Community Behavioral Healthcare, the Association of Behavioral Healthcare Management was formed in 1959 during the annual meeting of the American Psychiatric Association's Hospital and Community Psychiatry Institute. The organization represents a broad cross-section of professional healthcare managers that cares for a combined six million Americans who suffer from mental illnesses, developmental disabilities, and substance-abuse disorders. Members work in mental health, substance abuse, rehabilitation, housing, and community support services.

Canadian College of Health Service Executives

292 Somerset St. West
Ottawa, ON K2P 0J6
Canada
www.cchse.org

Founded in 1970, the Canadian College of Health Service Executives is a national, professional association that serves the needs of more than three thousand executives and senior managers from hospital, long-term-care, government, community health, teaching, home-care, consulting, and corporate sectors.

The college's mission is to provide leadership in the Canadian health system for excellence in health-services management by developing and promoting quality standards, research, certification, and professional development. The college is known for its credential of Certified Health Executive (CHE) and as the publisher of the quarterly journal *Healthcare Management FORUM*.

Canadian Public Health Association

1565 Carling Ave., Ste. 400

Ottawa, ON K1Z 8R1

Canada

www.cpha.ca

The Canadian Public Health Association (CPHA) is a national not-for-profit, voluntary association that encourages membership from all health-services groups and the public. CPHA is associated with eleven provincial/territorial public health branches and associations. CPHA undertakes programs in the areas of public health, health promotion and protection, and health public policy; publishes the *Canadian Journal of Public Health*; and is the sole agent in Canada for World Health Organization publications.

Medical Group Management Association

104 Inverness Terr. East

Englewood, CO 80112

www.mgma.com

A nonprofit corporation founded in 1926, the Medical Group Management Association (MGMA) is the oldest and largest organization in the field of medical group practice. MGMA's 19,500 members represent more than 240,000 group practice physicians internationally. MGMA's mission is to advance the art and science of medical practice management and to improve the health of our communities. The MGMA has two affiliated organizations: the MGMA Center for Research, founded in 1973, and the American College of Medical Practice Executives, founded in 1956.

National Association of Health Services Executives
8630 Fenton St., Ste. 126
Silver Spring, MD 20910
www.nahse.org

The National Association of Health Services Executives (NAHSE) was founded in 1968 in response to a challenge by the late Whitney M. Young Jr., executive director of the National Urban League, who called upon black and other minority health-services administrators to become involved in the promotion of quality health services to the poor and disadvantaged citizens of America. Since its founding, NAHSE has become involved in health careers programs, health administration education, health legislation and regulations, and a variety of community service projects. The organization is responsible for the creation of the Summer Work-Study Program (1970) that operated for eight years as a joint program of NAHSE and the Association of University Programs in Health Administration (AUPHA).

NAHSE has twenty chapters around the country. Membership is open to all persons interested in improvement of the quality of health services to minority and disadvantaged populations.

Selected Journals

American Journal of Public Health
American Public Health Association
800 I St. NW Washington, DC 20001
www.ajph.org
(monthly)

Contemporary Long-Term Care
HealthNet Information Services
120 Littleton Rd., Ste. 120
Parsippany, NJ 07054
www.cltcmag.com
(monthly)

Health Care Management Review
Lippincott Williams & Wilkins
530 Walnut St.
Philadelphia, PA 19106
www.hcmrjournal.com
(quarterly)

Health Progress
Catholic Health Association of the United States
4455 Woodson Rd.
St. Louis, MO 63134
www.chausa.org
(bimonthly)

Healthcare Executive
American College of Healthcare Executives
1 N. Franklin St., Ste. 1700
Chicago, IL 60606
www.ache.org/pubs/hcexecsub.cfm
(bimonthly)

Healthcare Financial Management
Healthcare Financial Management Association
2 Westbrook Corporate Center, Ste. 700
Westchester, IL 60154
www.hfma.org
(monthly)

Hospitals & Health Networks
Health Forum, Inc.
1 N. Franklin St.
Chicago, IL 60606
www.hhnmag.com
(monthly)

MGMA Connexion
Medical Group Management Association
104 Inverness Terr. East
Englewood, CO 80112
www.mgma.com/about/connexion.cfm
(ten times a year)

Modern Healthcare
Crain Communications
360 N. Michigan Ave., 5th Fl.
Chicago, IL 60601
www.modernhealthcare.com.
(weekly)

Sample Job Advertisements

You'll find job opportunities publicized on online job boards and institutions' websites and through university career centers, newspapers, and, most important, word-of-mouth. The following ads are typical of what you'll find online and in newspapers, and they offer some insight into the job demands, educational requirements, and career skills important to each position.

Senior Administrative Staff

Chief Executive Officer—Large Hospital

One of the nation's premier public, tertiary, teaching medical systems, affiliated with the University is recruiting qualified candidates for the senior executive position. The system, licensed for more than 1,000 beds, includes comprehensive, full-service acute, skilled, rehabilitation, ambulatory care and behavioral health services for the community and West Coast. XYZ is dedicated to a public, quality-driven mission and is embarking upon bold initiatives in preparing for its future through cost repositioning, partnerships with physicians and other providers, and organizational transformation.

Qualified candidates must have at least 10 years of progressively responsible senior executive experience in health care with accountability for, and proven success in, medical staff relations, organizational development and leadership, cost management, and quality. Appropriate academic credentials, including a preference for postgraduate degree, and teaching hospital experience in aligning physician and institutional interests in managed care and developing the infrastructure for effectively competing in aggressive markets, are sought. Innovative management experience in broad-based work redesign and participative change management is essential. A commitment to the organization's public mission with public accountability and experience in effective media relations and strong internal and external communications are required. XYZ is an equal opportunity employer.

The board of trustees will entertain résumés, through its consultant, until February 1. Please submit your résumé by mail to: Board of Trustees, Search Committee.

Chief Executive Officer—Small Hospital

XYZ Hospital, a small hospital located in the beautiful mountains, is seeking a chief executive officer to lead us into the 21st century.

This 25-bed hospital offers a range of inpatient and outpatient community services including emergency, outpatient surgery, physical therapy, and cardiac rehabilitation.

Candidates will have an in-depth knowledge of integrated health-care delivery systems with the ability to drive a strategic plan as well as have a strong background in hospital financial and budgetary principles. A bachelor's degree and a minimum of 5 years' experience in an administrative position within a hospital or health-care setting are mandatory for this position. A master's in health administration is preferred.

Competitive salary and benefit package complement the quality of lifestyle our rural location offers. If you are interested in this opportunity, please send a current résumé or CV along with salary history to: Board of Trustees, Search Committee.

XYZ Hospital is an equal opportunity employer and service provider.

Vice President, Operations

XYZ Memorial Hospital is seeking a candidate for the position of vice president. We are a strong and growing community hospital in an excellent location. The hospital is stable, well positioned, and offers comprehensive inpatient and outpatient services in an integrated network.

The successful candidate will have a M.H.A. or equivalent degree and at least 10 years of progressive experience demonstrating successful health-care management skills.

Chief Financial Officer

A 235-bed hospital in the Southeast has retained a firm to recruit for a new chief financial officer. This position is a member of the executive team and has significant impact on the future shape of the organization. Candidates must have strong decision-making abilities, good interpersonal skills, financial acumen, and the ability to effectively interact not only with medical staff but with board members as well.

Qualifications for this position include a bachelor's degree. A C.P.A. and master's are strongly preferred. Ideally the individual will have experience and exposure to a managed-care environment. This position offers an outstanding salary, benefits, and relocation package. Please mail résumés in confidence or fax to: Board of Trustees, Search Committee.

Chief Operating Officer

A well-respected and religiously sponsored regional health-care system is seeking a chief operating officer for a newly created position. Located in the Southwest, this position reports to the system's chief executive officer and is responsible for improving the competitive positioning of five operating units, reducing costs per adjusted discharge, and enhancing services that complement other elements of this emerging, integrated delivery network.

The successful candidate will assume leadership and management of large-scale transformational processes, including all the following: reengineering; implementation of a comprehensive information infrastructure; restructuring management systems and practices; and the alignment of hospital services with community needs in a market that is moving quickly to managed care.

Qualified candidates must have: an M.B.A, M.H.A., or related degree; 10+ years' health-care experience, with at least 3 years as an operations officer for a hospital or health system; proven success at transforming hospital operations to effectively meet the challenges of managed care/capitation; exceptional communication and interpersonal skills with the ability to effectively relate with individuals from a variety of ethnic and cultural backgrounds; strong values and beliefs, coupled with integrity, creativity, and a positive attitude.

An excellent compensation and benefits package, including a comprehensive relocation package, is provided.

Vice President, Nursing Service

We're seeking an individual who will bring vision and leadership to our full-service community hospital.

At XYZ Hospital, you'll be a member of the Top Corporation, one of the leading systems of health care. As a member of administration, you will be responsible to maintain and improve the delivery of efficient, cost-effective, quality care and patient services to the residents of coastal and surrounding communities.

As senior management, you will provide direction and leadership as you oversee operations of XYZ Hospital and develop/manage plans of care; identify business development opportunities; oversee development of partnerships; maintain effective and efficient operation of medical, surgical, ICU, dialysis, emergency, mental health, and Women's and Infants Center (140 beds); and ensure operational objectives remain consistent with the philosophy, mission, and strategic plan of XYZ Hospital.

The candidate we seek will hold a degree in nursing along with a master's degree in business, health care, or related field. Three to 5 years of progressive management experience to include all areas of hospital operations is required. Ability to work effectively with a diverse group of management, staff, and physicians is essential. In addition, proven skills in strategic planning, consensus building, coordinating quality improvement principles, and problem solving are necessary.

You will be compensated with a competitive salary and a flexible benefits package.

Coordinator, Quality Management

XYZ Hospital seeks a self-directed individual to coordinate quality management functions including medical staff & hospitalwide quality improvement, data collection/evaluation, & work injury mgt. Two years' hospital-based clinical experience (preferably in psych. or PM&R) required; 1 year utilization review/quality improvement experience, PA licensed R.N., and/or CPHQ preferred. We offer a generous compensation package as well as free parking.

Director, Patient Financial Services

The position will report to the system VP finance and be responsible for 150 FTEs in credit, collections, billing, and admissions. Preferred candidates will have 5+ years' management experience in patient finance with a C.P.A./M.B.A. preferred. Experience in effective management of multisite operations is highly desired.

An extremely competitive compensation and relocation package is available.

Director, Management Information Systems

Responsibilities entail direct supervision and management of our management information systems function. The requirements include strong interpersonal and organizational skills with management in a sophisticated information systems operation. A B.S. in computer science or related field required. A strong preference will be given to candidates with a master's-level education, HBOC or UNIX experience, and/or experience in the development of integrated health-care delivery systems.

Director, Marketing

Located in the hills near a prominent New England hospital, this leader in chemical dependency treatment for adults and adolescents seeks aggressive director of marketing. Will be responsible for planning, organizing, and leading and developing regional marketing/sales staff. Must have marketing management exp., background in managed-care contracting, and successful track record in sales. Competitive compensation program plus benefits. We offer a high quality of life and no state income or sales tax.

Director, Planning

XYZ Health System, the second-largest health-care delivery system in central U.S., is seeking a director of planning.

XYZ Health System comprises three hospitals (462-bed tertiary care center/teaching hospital, 287-bed acute care hospital, and 194-bed community hospital); primary care MSO/physician network, specialty PHO, ambulatory/primary care centers; home care, hospice, and medical transportation services.

The director of planning will report to the VP of planning and marketing and will be responsible for strategic business planning activities for various business units throughout our growing delivery system. This position will work closely with peers in strategic planning, market research, business development, and regional network developments to develop action-oriented business plans and coordinate the development of new markets, products, and services. Candidates must possess a master's degree in business or health-care administration, marketing, social sciences, or a related field and have 5 years' experience in planning/business development in an integrated or regional health-care system.

At XYZ Health System, we are devoted to the personal and professional growth of our associates in an empowering, team-oriented, and progressive environment. We offer a competitive compensation and benefits package.

Director, Public Affairs

XYZ Hospital, a leading Midwest not-for-profit health-care organization, seeks an experienced, self-motivated professional with exceptional organizational and communication skills to:

- Oversee marketing/public relations staff
- Direct foundation's fund development initiatives

- Manage five off-site family medicine practices
- Negotiate managed-care contracts
- Develop hospital sponsored preferred provider product

Position reports to the CEO and is a member of the six-person executive leadership team. Candidate must possess M.B.A. or M.H.A. with 5+ years' experience preferred. Excellent and comprehensive compensation and benefits package offered. A brief statement of why you are best prepared to meet the rigors of this position will accompany the résumé of the successful candidate.

Support Services

Director, Purchasing

Enjoy living in an area with an easygoing lifestyle, low crime rate, clean air, and plenty of wide-open space? XYZ Memorial Hospital, a progressive 76-bed hospital located in a year-round resort area, has a full-time opening for a director of purchasing. Bachelor's degree or comparable experience. Sufficient previous experience in purchasing, receiving, distribution, and stores. Health-care experience preferred. Competitive salary and benefits. Deep Creek Lake and the Wisp Ski Resort are just a few of the many recreational offerings available.

Director, Human Resources/Assistant Administrator

Successful Southeastern Community Hospital Seeking Director of Human Resources/Assistant Administrator. This is a rewarding position for an individual who is well organized and a self-starter. Requires administrative direction of support departments within the facility as well as all aspects of personnel management. Spanish, as first or second language, necessary. Salary compatible with blended duties.

Psychiatric Administrator

The leading provider of inpatient and outpatient psychiatric services in south-central U.S. seeks an experienced administrator to direct and develop a comprehensive system of mental-health care. The XYZ Center is a freestanding psychiatric hospital with office complex on-site and several outpatient/outreach clinics throughout the region. Near Gulf Coast or Atlantic beaches. Interested candidates must have either M.H.A. or M.B.A. with experience in both inpatient and outpatient services administration and should be committed to innovation, leadership, and market dominance.

Administrator, Insurance Managed Care

Our client is a large national HMO with a strong financial foundation and commitment. We are seeking an individual with proven management skills in sales and operations, as well as someone capable of building long-term relationships with national accounts, brokers, and consultants.

Manager, Managed Care

Since 1900 XYZ Insurance Companies has been providing comprehensive, superior insurance protection and related services to select business owners, trade associations, and buying groups. Today we are a highly respected, multiple-line company with $2.4 billion in assets, $804 million in premiums, and 2,600 employees. Our continued success and growth have prompted our search for an individual to direct the planning, development, and marketing of managed health-care products and services that assist client policyholders in effectively managing cost and quality. This position is located in our home office in the Midwest.

Qualifications include:

- Minimum 4-year college degree in business administration, marketing, health-care management, or related field
- Minimum 5 to 7 years in managed-care-administration-related work experience
- Excellent communication, organization, and negotiating skills

We offer a professional work environment, comprehensive benefits program, and a salary that is commensurate with education and experience.

Health-Care Risk Manager, Outside Firm

The XYZ Group, a provider of insurance and risk-management services to the health-care industry, is seeking an experienced risk manager to lead the department. Our clientele includes both individual health-care providers and health-care facilities. Applicants must have a clinical background. Legal training or experience is highly preferred. The successful candidate will have excellent managerial skills; experience with Power Point, Word, and Excel; and the ability to communicate effectively. The candidate will develop and present training programs to health-care professionals, as well as survey health-care facilities throughout the country. Master's degree and 5 to 7 years' related experience required. The XYZ Group offers a friendly, professional work environment and competitive compensation and benefits package.

Health-Care Chief Operating Officer, Group Practice

Rapidly growing multisite physician group practice in the Northeast offers an immediate opportunity for a hands-on chief operating officer. Reporting directly to the president/CEO, this professional must have a strong understanding of physician practices as well as a history of growing practice revenues. Experience in managed-care risk contracts and knowledge of most current information systems required.

Our expanding organization offers an excellent compensation and benefits package.

Director of Compliance

XYZ Group services Fortune 500 companies with a full range of products and services. The compliance director in our health-care group will:

- Develop, recommend, and lead the implementation of appropriate regulatory compliance policies and procedures ensuring integrity in responding to complaints, issues, and regulatory events
- Create the tools and practices to ensure an accurate and complete response to all regulatory events, market conducts, reviews, and so on, and minimize risk and legal exposure
- Provide direction and interpretation for legislation and direct processes for appropriate implementation and adoption by business areas
- Foster effective use of monitoring and tracking process to ensure implementation of new mandates by business and effective company response to unacceptable risks related to new legislation
- Face out to regulatory agencies as needed at both the state and federal level to ensure accurate understanding and legal interpretation

Qualifications: Advanced degree preferred. B.S. degree in business, systems, health care; master's or equivalent experience desired. 8+ years process consulting, audit experience, or six sigma background. Regulatory/compliance background desired. Business acumen, strong communication skills, influencing and negotiation skills desired. Equal-opportunity employer.

Marketing

Health-Care Consultant

XYZ Solutions thru Technology (STT), a division of XYZ Corporation, is experiencing rapid growth in the Southeast and has a variety of challenging coastal opportunities.

Practice Leader/Management Level

Will act as market leader responsible for business development, strategic planning, implementation, and delivery. Prior managed-care, insurance, "Big 6" consulting, or software application development experience with a major software vendor a plus. Health-care background required.

Senior- or Associate-Level Consultant

Must have strong background in client/server technologies and system implementation. Health-care experience and market development capabilities a plus.

We offer a competitive salary and benefits package. For confidential consideration or more information, please send your résumé to: Staffing.

Director of Development, Public Relations

Primary duties and responsibilities: Direct and supervise current giving activities and develop strategies to secure gifts. Develop and recommend goals and objectives for fund-raising, implementing campaigns, techniques, and department policies to achieve such goals. Conduct research and maintain records on gift potential of corporations/organizations and individuals. Develop budgets and goals in coordination with executive director of XYZ Health

Foundation. Participate in the design of campaigns as approved by the foundation to meet priority needs of the hospital and college. Coordinate and attend fund-raising benefits for the foundation. Provide information to key prospects and donors through newsletters, mailings, and foundation updates. Must maintain active involvement in at least one community organization that links to the overall mission of XYZ's Health Foundation.

Qualifications: Bachelor's degree preferred and a minimum of 3 to 5 years of fund-raising experience. The ideal candidate will have the ability to identify, research, and cultivate donors and prospects. Must have excellent communication abilities both spoken and written and a high energy level.

President, Medical Services Organization

XYZ Inc., a fast-growing health-care industry leader based in the Southeast, is seeking a highly motivated senior executive who has hands-on experience in managing a start-up HMO/PPO company. Qualified candidates must possess an advanced degree—preferably one that is health-care related, a min. of 8 years' senior mgt. experience, and an in-depth knowledge of negotiating contracts for IPAs in several markets. Proven success with physician practice mgt. is required.

The ideal candidate should be able to manage and develop staff to take this division to a $250M revenue base and generate acceptable profit margins. Position reports to the chief operating officer. Excellent relocation and benefit package available, which includes stock options, 401(k) with matching and immediate vesting, and insurance.

Director, Medical Group Practice

Successful, highly respected, multispecialty medical group in California seeks executive director to lead organization into the next century. Qualifications include minimum of 10 years' health-care experience in an increasingly responsible management position; proven record of success in managing people in a complex, competitive environment; outstanding leadership and communication skills; and ability to attract and retain outstanding individuals to form a strong administrative team.

Successful candidate will assume overall responsibility for planning and administration of all nonclinical activities of the medical group. Reports directly to the board of directors and is ultimately responsible for the continued growth and success of the organization.

XYZ Group Inc. has served patients and businesses in the San Francisco Bay area for more than 40 years. With multiple locations in Silicon Valley between San Jose and San Francisco, its 160 physicians and 750 employees enjoy a wide range of recreational, cultural, and lifestyle opportunities. We offer an outstanding benefit and compensation package, with future increases linked directly to performance.

Manager, Data Services—Informatics

The selected applicant will define and implement data policies and strategies in support of Informatics and Disease Management Informatics strategic plan. This person will also define, implement, and support the Informatics strategic database architecture and its associated environments and participate in shaping companywide data architecture. A B.A./B.S. or relevant experience plus 10 years' related work experience in data management and/or applications development required. Also must have a minimum of 3 years' experience in a supervisory/management role and large, multiple database (>200GB) management and design experience.

Elderly Services

Administrator, Nursing Services

Seeking licensed NHA for 100-bed nonprofit facility in Northeast area. This person must have minimum of 3 yrs. experience in LTC. B.S. or master's degree. Must have excellent communication skills, be take-charge person, and have strong work ethic. Individual must be flexible, caring person who enjoys working with elderly and their families on daily basis.

Executive Director

XYZ Nurse Home Health Service, a leading home-health-care agency with approximately 240 employees, has an exceptional opportunity for an experienced director.

Requirements include a bachelor's degree in management, business administration, nursing, or other closely related field. A master's degree is helpful but not essential. Five years of progressive management responsibility in a service organization. Home-care or health-care experience desirable.

This position requires leadership responsive to the changing needs of health care.

About the Author

I. Donald Snook Jr. was a nationally renowned leader in hospital management and marketing and president of the Presbyterian Foundation for Philadelphia. He also served as CEO of Presbyterian Medical Center of Philadelphia.

Snook contributed numerous articles to health-care management literature and wrote several books, including the widely read *Hospitals: What They Are and How They Work*. He created the "hotel-hospital" concept. He received the American Healthcare Marketing Association's CEO Marketer of the Year award and the Senior Regent award from the American College of Healthcare Executives, Southeastern Pennsylvania region.

Snook graduated cum laude with a B.B.A. in marketing from the Wharton School at the University of Pennsylvania and earned an M.B.A. in hospital administration from George Washington University. He also completed the Health Management Systems Program at the Harvard Business School.

More recently, Snook was a faculty member in the graduate program in health-care administration at LaSalle University and Pennsylvania State University and a fellow in the American College of Healthcare Executives. Snook conducted seminars nationally on contemporary issues. He died in November 2002.

The editors would like to thank Brad Crawford for preparing this edition.